POLITICS AND ECONOMICS OF THE MIDDLE EAST

G000128548

CORRUPTION, CONTRACTORS, AND WARLORDS IN AFGHANISTAN

POLITICS AND ECONOMICS OF THE MIDDLE EAST

Additional books in this series can be found on Nova's website under the Series tab.

Additional E-books in this series can be found on Nova's website under the E-books tab.

DEFENSE, SECURITY AND STRATEGIES

Additional books in this series can be found on Nova's website under the Series tab.

Additional E-books in this series can be found on Nova's website under the E-books tab.

POLITICS AND ECONOMICS OF THE MIDDLE EAST

CORRUPTION, CONTRACTORS, AND WARLORDS IN AFGHANISTAN

JACOB E. JANKOWSKI
EDITOR

Nova Science Publishers, Inc.
New York

Copyright © 2011 by Nova Science Publishers, Inc.

All rights reserved. No part of this book may be reproduced, stored in a retrieval system or transmitted in any form or by any means: electronic, electrostatic, magnetic, tape, mechanical photocopying, recording or otherwise without the written permission of the Publisher.

For permission to use material from this book please contact us:
Telephone 631-231-7269; Fax 631-231-8175
Web Site: http://www.novapublishers.com

NOTICE TO THE READER

The Publisher has taken reasonable care in the preparation of this book, but makes no expressed or implied warranty of any kind and assumes no responsibility for any errors or omissions. No liability is assumed for incidental or consequential damages in connection with or arising out of information contained in this book. The Publisher shall not be liable for any special, consequential, or exemplary damages resulting, in whole or in part, from the readers' use of, or reliance upon, this material. Any parts of this book based on government reports are so indicated and copyright is claimed for those parts to the extent applicable to compilations of such works.

Independent verification should be sought for any data, advice or recommendations contained in this book. In addition, no responsibility is assumed by the publisher for any injury and/or damage to persons or property arising from any methods, products, instructions, ideas or otherwise contained in this publication.

This publication is designed to provide accurate and authoritative information with regard to the subject matter covered herein. It is sold with the clear understanding that the Publisher is not engaged in rendering legal or any other professional services. If legal or any other expert assistance is required, the services of a competent person should be sought. FROM A DECLARATION OF PARTICIPANTS JOINTLY ADOPTED BY A COMMITTEE OF THE AMERICAN BAR ASSOCIATION AND A COMMITTEE OF PUBLISHERS.

Additional color graphics may be available in the e-book version of this book.

LIBRARY OF CONGRESS CATALOGING-IN-PUBLICATION DATA

Corruption, contractors, and warlords in Afghanistan / editor, Jacob E. Jankowski.
p. cm.
Includes index.
ISBN 978-1-61761-598-6 (hardcover)
1. United States--Armed Forces--Procurement. 2. Corruption--Afghanistan.
3. Private military companies--Afghanistan. 4. Contracting out--United States. 5. Afghan War, 2001---Logistics. I. Jankowski, Jacob E.
UC263.C68 2010
958.104'7--dc22
2010033046

Published by Nova Science Publishers, Inc. † New York

CONTENTS

PREFACE

In Afghanistan, the U.S. military faces one of the most complicated and difficult supply chains in the history of warfare. The task of feeding, fueling, and arming American troops at over 200 forward operating bases and combat outposts sprinkled across a difficult and hostile terrain with only minimal road infrastructure is nothing short of herculean. In order to accomplish this mission, the Department of Defense employs a hitherto unprecedented logistics model: responsibility for the supply chain is almost entirely outsourced to local truckers and Afghan private security providers. The principal contract supporting the U.S. supply chain in Afghanistan is called the Host Nation Trucking (HNT), a $2.16 billion contract split among eight Afghan, American, and Middle Eastern companies. This book explores the potential strategic consequences of supply chain contracting in Afghanistan

Chapter 1- In November 2009, at the behest of Chairman John Tierney, the Majority staff of the Subcommittee on National Security and Foreign Affairs initiated a preliminary inquiry into the Department of Defense's Afghan Host Nation Trucking (HNT) contract. This inquiry was prompted by a report from Aram Roston in *The Nation*[1] regarding allegations that U.S. trucking contractors were making protection payments for safe passage through insecure areas in order to supply U.S. troops in the field. In December 2009, Chairman Tierney sent letters to the Department of Defense and to the eight HNT contractors requesting documents and information related to the operation of the contract. In total, the Department and the contractors produced over 25,000 pages of documents to Chairman Tierney and Ranking Member Jeff Flake.

After receiving documents, Majority and Minority staff formally interviewed 31 witnesses in connection with the investigation, including military personnel, HNT contractors, private security providers, and experts on politics and corruption in Afghanistan. The Majority staff recorded detailed notes from each meeting and subsequently provided memoranda summarizing individual interviews to the Minority staff for comment. Those interview memoranda are on file with the Subcommittee. The Majority staff conducted preliminary interviews with three senior Department of Defense officials referenced in this chapter but were prohibited from conducting formal interviews by the Department's decision to resist access to military personnel deployed in Afghanistan.

The Majority and Minority staff also received several relevant intelligence briefings, but, for purposes of public dissemination, no classified information is contained in this chapter.

Due to the security risks faced by contractor personnel supporting the U.S. mission in Afghanistan, this chapter does not specifically disclose the names or identities of many cooperating witnesses.

Chapter 2- In our constitutional democracy, Congress is charged with overseeing that the Executive Branch executes its responsibilities in accordance with law. Toward that end, this Congress has invested the Subcommittee on National Security and Foreign Affairs with a clear mandate to root out waste, fraud, and abuse, wherever we may find it.

Real oversight is a powerful tool for transparency and accountability, not for political grandstanding. Today's report by the Majority staff represents the best tradition of constructive oversight. After six months, 31 witnesses, 25,000 documents, hundreds of hours of work, and, yes, even tea with one of the warlords at the heart of the investigation, the report provides the Subcommittee, the Congress, and the American people with significant insight into how the Department of Defense has managed the supply chain for U.S. troops in Afghanistan.

An investigation of this nature is akin to a puzzle. We have laboriously gathered the pieces on the table, fit together the edges, and filled in enough sections for us to understand what the picture will look like, but there are still portions to be completed. Though the puzzle is unfinished, and important questions remain, the portrait that emerges is of the Department of Defense's systematic failure of management and oversight of contractors along the Afghan supply chain.

In the past eight years, the United States has placed an enormous burden on our brave men and women in uniform. The military has been asked to fight two grueling conflicts in some of the most difficult and hostile conditions imaginable. The challenge of supplying our troops in the field is simply staggering.

Chapter 3- Chairman Tierney – Congressman Flake – Distinguished Members of the Subcommittee on National Security and Foreign Affairs. Thank you for this opportunity to discuss the role of the United States Army in the Department of Defense's Management and Oversight of the Host Nation Trucking Contract in Afghanistan. I am pleased to represent Army leadership, the more than 40,000 members of the Army Acquisition and Contracting Workforce, and the more than one million Soldiers who have deployed to combat over the last eight and a half years and who have trusted us to provide them with materiel, supplies, and services in the right place, at the right time.

Mr. Chairman, I had the privilege of serving as the Commanding General of the Joint Contracting Command-Iraq/Afghanistan just prior to taking on my present duties and responsibilities. Although my office was in Baghdad, I traveled frequently throughout Iraq and Afghanistan. Let me state at the outset that the Host Nation Trucking contract is absolutely vital to the sustainment of our forces in Afghanistan. Contracting for, obtaining, and overseeing services in an austere environment, in a fragile economy with a poor financial system, limited rule of law, and during hostilities is a dangerous and difficult task that is being performed daily throughout Afghanistan in spite of these immense challenges.

Chapter 4- Chairman Tierney, Ranking Member Flake, and members of the Committee, thank you for the opportunity to appear before you today to discuss the program management and oversight of private security contracts.

As the Quadrennial Defense Review (QDR) acknowledged, contractors are part of the total force, providing an adaptable mix of unique skill sets, local knowledge, and flexibility that a strictly military force cannot cultivate or resource for all scenarios. Contractors provide a broad range of supplies, services, and critical logistics support in many capability areas, while reducing the military footprint and increasing the availability and readiness of resources. Typically, there is a higher reliance on contracted support during the post-conflict phases of an operation (Phase IV- Stabilization and Phase V - Enable Civil Authority).

Current operations in the U.S. Central Command (USCENTCOM) Area of Operations require Private Security Contractors (PSCs) to fulfill a variety of important security functions for the Department of Defense (DoD), the Department of State (DoS), and other U.S. Government (USG) entities supporting Operation IRAQI FREEDOM and Operation ENDURING FREEDOM. Relief, recovery, and reconstruction of a post-conflict region are traditionally civilian functions, and thus it is entirely appropriate for civilian resources to be used to protect these activities from theft, extortion, vandalism, terrorism, and other unlawful violence. DoD contracts with PSCs to protect personnel, facilities, and activities. The roles of PSCs are analogous to civilian security guard forces, not combat forces. By using civilian resources to accomplish selected civilian tasks, military forces can focus on the military mission.

Chapter 5- Chairman Tierney, Ranking Member Flake, and members of the Committee, thank you for the opportunity to appear before you today to discuss DoD's efforts to link contracting and the flow of US government contracting funds to a winning counterinsurgency strategy in Afghanistan.

The focus of the counterinsurgency (COIN) strategy in Afghanistan is the Afghan people. We are focused on population-centric counterinsurgency operations: enabling an expanded and effective Afghan National Security Force, securing the population, and connecting the Government of Afghanistan to its people by supporting improved governance and economic development. The effects that US government contracting funds are having on the battlefield have not always contributed to the success of our strategy. Optimizing the effects of our contracting dollars in support of COIN objectives is crucial to our success.

In fiscal year 2009, the US Government spent more than $8.6 billion on contracts with a place of work in Afghanistan, of which more than $7 billion were awarded by DoD. In some cases, segments of the Afghan populace and government perceive that this money is not positively benefiting the Afghan people, and is supporting power brokers and malign actors. This is obviously not our intent nor in our strategic interest.

Chapter 6- Chairman Tierney, Ranking Member Flake, distinguished members of the subcommittee, thank you for the opportunity to appear before you today to discuss the Department of Defense's use of Private Security Contractors in Afghanistan.

The Department of Defense (DOD) is just one of many entities—including other U.S. government agencies, foreign governments, international organizations, and private industry—that employ private security contractors (PSC) in Afghanistan. In recent years, the United States and many other nations and organizations, have increasingly turned to private contractors to provide security, as well as a variety of other functions, in support of stabilization and reconstruction efforts.[1] This increased reliance on contractors has fueled the growth of the private security industry worldwide.

Chapter 7- A strong personality-driven political order is emerging in Afghanistan which undermines ISAF's goals. This chapter discusses the historical context of governance structures in Kandahar, the declining influençe of tribes, Kandahar's current powerbrokers, and the rise of the Karzai family.

Kandahar is strategic terrain for the Quetta Shura Taliban and the Karzai family, and a central focus of ISAF's 2010 counterinsurgency campaign.

Ahmed Wali Karzai's influence over Kandahar is the central obstacle to any of ISAF's governance objectives, and a consistent policy for dealing with him must be a central element of any new strategy. Wali Karzai's behavior and waning popularity among local populations promote instability and provide space for the Taliban to exist.

ISAF has inadvertently strengthened the forces that undermine legitimate government institutions. ISAF must shape the political landscape in Kandahar so that the local government becomes a credible partner.

ISAF must develop a new coherent strategy that is unified in both Kandahar and Kabul and that recognizes the means by which informal power structures co-opt and undermine the development of robust institutions.

A new ISAF strategy must include:

Unity of effort among coalition actors at the national and provincial levels.

Comprehensive intelligence on the interests and relationships of local powerbrokers, contracting networks, and on the connections between Kabul and Kandahar.

Reform of ISAF contracting, to ensure distribution of ISAF funding to a broad range of constituencies, and to ensure that contracts do not create strong military-commercials networks.

Disarmament and demobilization of private security forces and private militias.

Building ministerial capacity in Kandahar and Kabul to ensure strong and independent security forces.

Chapter 8- In Iraq and Afghanistan, the use of contractors has reached a level unprecedented in U.S. military operations. In September 2009, contractors represented 47% of DOD's workforce in Iraq and 62% in Afghanistan.[1] The presence of contractors on the battlefield is obviously not a new phenomenon but decisions made over the last few decades have dramatically increased DoD's reliance on them to execute its basic missions. First, force structure reductions ranging from the post-Vietnam decisions to move the majority of Army logistics support elements to the Army Reserve and Guard[2] to the post-Cold War reduction in force decisions that reduced the

Army from 18 to 10 divisions greatly reduced the services' ability to support long-term operations. Next came a series of decisions that led to the wider employment of contractors in the Balkans during the 1990s. Finally, the decision to invade Iraq with a minimum of force left the U.S. with too few troops to deal with the disorder that resulted from the removal of the regime. Thus it is understandable that given the immediate, unanticipated need for large numbers of logistics and security personnel, the shortage of such troops on active duty and the precedent for using contractors in the Balkans, the Pentagon turned to contractors to fill the immediate needs. However, the subsequent failure to conduct a careful analysis of the wisdom of using contractors is less understandable. For the purposes of this chapter, the services provided by private contractors will include both armed and unarmed services. While the U.S. government has conducted and continues to conduct numerous investigations into fraud, waste and corruption in the contracting process, it has not yet systematically explored the essential question -- "Is it strategically a good idea to use contractors in counterinsurgency operations or even military operations in general?"

Chapter 9- The Subcommittee has expressed concern over the practice of making payments to local warlords and even Taliban forces to secure the transit of goods through the territories they control. Opponents of the practice see it as corrupt in principle and an unnecessary acknowledgment of the Taliban's authority in areas of primary concern to the US/NATO campaign. Defenders see it instead as a necessary means of securing a greater end, namely, the advancement of the current strategy of gaining control over territories, holding them, and then promoting forms of development that the local population will welcome. In this light, the practice becomes as tactical means of making the Taliban complicit in its own destruction as an effective force.

In: Corruption, Contractors, and Warlords… ISBN: 978-1-61761-598-6
Editor: Jacob E. Jankowski © 2011 Nova Science Publishers, Inc.

Chapter 1

WARLORD, INC.: EXTORTION AND CORRUPTION ALONG THE U.S. SUPPLY CHAIN IN AFGHANISTAN

John F. Tierney

NOTE ON METHODOLOGY

In November 2009, at the behest of Chairman John Tierney, the Majority staff of the Subcommittee on National Security and Foreign Affairs initiated a preliminary inquiry into the Department of Defense's Afghan Host Nation Trucking (HNT) contract. This inquiry was prompted by a report from Aram Roston in *The Nation*[1] regarding allegations that U.S. trucking contractors were making protection payments for safe passage through insecure areas in order to supply U.S. troops in the field. In December 2009, Chairman Tierney sent letters to the Department of Defense and to the eight HNT contractors requesting documents and information related to the operation of the contract. In total, the Department and the contractors produced over 25,000 pages of documents to Chairman Tierney and Ranking Member Jeff Flake.

After receiving documents, Majority and Minority staff formally interviewed 31 witnesses in connection with the investigation, including military personnel, HNT contractors, private security providers, and experts on politics and corruption in Afghanistan. The Majority staff recorded detailed notes from each meeting and subsequently provided memoranda summarizing individual interviews to the Minority staff for comment. Those interview memoranda are on file with the Subcommittee. The Majority staff conducted preliminary interviews with three senior Department of Defense officials referenced in this chapter but were prohibited from conducting formal interviews by the Department's decision to resist access to military personnel deployed in Afghanistan.

The Majority and Minority staff also received several relevant intelligence briefings, but, for purposes of public dissemination, no classified information is contained in this chapter.

Due to the security risks faced by contractor personnel supporting the U.S. mission in Afghanistan, this chapter does not specifically disclose the names or identities of many cooperating witnesses.

With some important exceptions, the Subcommittee eventually received substantial cooperation with its investigation from the Department of Defense and most of the HNT contractors. Notably, after almost six months of requests, the Department only provided a critically relevant document relating to its own investigation into the allegations at issue on June 14, 2010 – eight days before the scheduled hearing on the Subcommittee's investigation. That document has been withheld from inclusion in this chapter at the Department of Defense's request. At the time of printing, discussions regarding the origin and context of that document are ongoing.

I. Executive Summary

We have to do a better job in the international side to coordinate our aid, to get more accountability for what we spend in Afghanistan. But much of the corruption is fueled by money that has poured into that country over the last eight years. And it is corruption at every step along the way, not just in Kabul.

You know, when we are so dependent upon long supply lines, as in Afghanistan, where everything has to be imported, it's much more difficult than it was in Iraq, where we had Kuwait as a staging ground to go into Iraq. You offload a ship in Karachi and by the time whatever it is – you know, muffins for our soldiers' breakfasts or anti-IED equipment – gets to where we're headed, it goes through a lot of hands. ***And one of the major sources of funding for the Taliban is the protection money.***

– Secretary of State Hillary Rodham Clinton
Testimony before the Senate Foreign Relations Committee
December 3, 2009

In Afghanistan, the U.S. military faces one of the most complicated and difficult supply chains in the history of warfare. The task of feeding, fueling, and arming American troops at over 200 forward operating bases and combat outposts sprinkled across a difficult and hostile terrain with only minimal road infrastructure is nothing short of herculean. In order to accomplish this mission, the Department of Defense employs a hitherto unprecedented logistics model: responsibility for the supply chain is almost entirely outsourced to local truckers and Afghan private security providers.

The principal contract supporting the U.S. supply chain in Afghanistan is called Host Nation Trucking, a $2.16 billion contract split among eight Afghan, American, and Middle Eastern companies. Although there are other supply chain contracts, the HNT contract provides trucking for over 70 percent of the total goods and materiel distributed to U.S. troops in the field, roughly 6,000 to 8,000 truck missions per month. The trucks carry food, supplies, fuel, ammunition, and even Mine Resistant Ambush Protected vehicles (MRAPs).

The crucial component of the HNT contract is that the prime contractors are responsible for the security of the cargo that they carry. Most of the prime contractors and their trucking subcontractors hire local Afghan security providers for armed protection of the trucking convoys. Transporting valuable and sensitive supplies in highly remote and insecure locations requires extraordinary levels of security. A typical convoy of 300 supply trucks going from Kabul to Kandahar, for example, will travel with 400 to 500 guards in dozens of trucks armed with heavy machine guns and rocket-propelled grenades (RPGs).

The private security companies that protect the convoys are frequently involved in armed conflict with alleged insurgents, rival security providers, and other criminal elements. The security providers report having lost hundreds of men over the course of the last year alone, though the veracity of these reports is difficult to judge. Many of the firefights purportedly last for hours and involve significant firepower and frequent civilian casualties. Indeed, in an interview with the Subcommittee staff, the leading convoy security commander in Afghanistan said that he spent $1.5 million on ammunition *per month*.

From one perspective, the HNT contract works quite well: the HNT providers supply almost all U.S. forward operating bases and combat outposts across a difficult and hostile terrain while only rarely needing the assistance of U.S. troops. Nearly all of the risk on the supply chain is borne by contractors, their local Afghan truck drivers, and the private security companies that defend them. During the Soviet Union's occupation of Afghanistan (1979-

1989), by contrast, its army devoted a substantial portion of its total force structure to defending its supply chain. The HNT contract allows the United States to dedicate a greater proportion of its troops to other counterinsurgency priorities instead of logistics.

But outsourcing the supply chain in Afghanistan to contractors has also had significant unintended consequences. The HNT contract fuels warlordism, extortion, and corruption, and it may be a significant source of funding for insurgents. In other words, the logistics contract has an outsized strategic impact on U.S. objectives in Afghanistan.

The Department of Defense has been largely blind to the potential strategic consequences of its supply chain contingency contracting. U.S. military logisticians have little visibility into what happens to their trucks on the road and virtually no understanding of how security is actually provided. When HNT contractors self-reported to the military that they were being extorted by warlords for protection payments for safe passage and that these payments were "funding the insurgency," they were largely met with indifference and inaction.

Specifically, the Subcommittee on National Security and Foreign Affairs Majority staff makes the following findings:

1. **Security for the U.S. Supply Chain Is Principally Provided by Warlords**. The principal private security subcontractors on the HNT contract are warlords, strongmen, commanders, and militia leaders who compete with the Afghan central government for power and authority. Providing "protection" services for the U.S. supply chain empowers these warlords with money, legitimacy, and a *raison d'etre* for their private armies. Although many of these warlords nominally operate under private security companies licensed by the Afghan Ministry of Interior, they thrive in a vacuum of government authority and their interests are in fundamental conflict with U.S. aims to build a strong Afghan government.
2. **The Highway Warlords Run a Protection Racket.** The HNT contractors and their trucking subcontractors in Afghanistan pay tens of millions of dollars annually to local warlords across Afghanistan in exchange for "protection" for HNT supply convoys to support U.S. troops. Although the warlords do provide guards and coordinate security, the contractors have little choice but to use them in what amounts to a vast protection racket. The consequences are clear: trucking companies that pay the highway warlords for security are

provided protection; trucking companies that do not pay believe they are more likely to find themselves under attack. As a result, almost everyone pays. In interviews and documents, the HNT contractors frequently referred to such payments as "extortion," "bribes," "special security," and/or "protection payments."

3. **Protection Payments for Safe Passage Are a Significant Potential Source of Funding for the Taliban.** Within the HNT contractor community, many believe that the highway warlords who provide security in turn make protection payments to insurgents to coordinate safe passage. This belief is evidenced in numerous documents, incident reports, and e-mails that refer to attempts at Taliban extortion along the road. The Subcommittee staff has not uncovered any direct evidence of such payments and a number of witnesses, including Ahmed Wali Karzai, all adamantly deny that any convoy security commanders pay insurgents. According to experts and public reporting, however, the Taliban regularly extort rents from a variety of licit and illicit industries, and it is plausible that the Taliban would try to extort protection payments from the coalition supply chain that runs through territory in which they freely operate.
4. **Unaccountable Supply Chain Security Contractors Fuel Corruption.** HNT contractors and their private security providers report widespread corruption by Afghan officials and frequent government extortion along the road. The largest private security provider for HNT trucks complained that it had to pay $1,000 to $10,000 in monthly bribes to nearly every Afghan governor, police chief, and local military unit whose territory the company passed. HNT contractors themselves reported similar corruption at a smaller scale, including significant numbers of Afghan National Police checkpoints. U.S. military officials confirmed that they were aware of these problems.
5. **Unaccountable Supply Chain Security Contractors Undermine U.S. Counterinsurgency Strategy.** While outsourcing principal responsibility for the supply chain in Afghanistan to local truckers and unknown security commanders has allowed the Department of Defense to devote a greater percentage of its force structure to priority operations, these logistics arrangements have significant unintended consequences for the overall counterinsurgency strategy. By fueling government corruption and funding parallel power structures, these

logistics arrangements undercut efforts to establish popular confidence in a credible and sustainable Afghan government.

6. **The Department of Defense Lacks Effective Oversight of Its Supply Chain and Private Security Contractors in Afghanistan.** The Department of Defense has little to no visibility into what happens to the trucks carrying U.S. supplies between the time they leave the gate to the time they arrive at their destination. Despite serious concerns regarding operations, no military managers have ever observed truck operations on the road or met with key security providers. The Department of Defense's regulations, promulgated in response to direction by Congress, require oversight of all private security companies working as contractors or subcontractors for the U.S government. These requirements include ensuring that all private security company personnel comply with U.S. government and local country firearm laws, that all private security company equipment be tracked, and that all incidents of death, injury, or property damage be fully investigated. The Department of Defense is grossly out of compliance with applicable regulations and has no visibility into the operations of the private security companies that are subcontractors on the HNT contract.
7. **HNT Contractors Warned the Department of Defense About Protection Payments for Safe Passage to No Avail.** In meetings, interviews, e-mails, white papers, and PowerPoint presentations, many HNT prime contractors self-reported to military officials and criminal investigators that they were being forced to make "protection payments for safe passage" on the road. While military officials acknowledged receiving the warnings, these concerns were never appropriately addressed.

There are numerous constructive changes that could be made to the U.S. military trucking effort in Afghanistan that would improve contracting integrity while mitigating corrupting influences. As the Department of Defense absorbs the findings in this chapter and considers its course of action, the Subcommittee on National Security and Foreign Affairs Majority staff makes the following recommendations:

1. **Assume Direct Contractual Responsibility for Supply Chain Security Providers.** If the United States is going to use small armies of private security contractors to defend its massive supply chain in a

war zone, the Department of Defense must take direct responsibility for those contractors to ensure robust oversight. Trucking companies are wholly incapable of overseeing this scale of security operations. The U.S. government needs to have a direct line of authority and accountability over the private security companies that guard the supply chain.

2. **Review Counterinsurgency Consequences of the HNT Contract.** The Department of Defense needs to conduct a top-to-bottom evaluation of the secondary effects of the HNT contract that includes an analysis of corruption, Afghan politics and power dynamics, military utility, and economic effects.
3. **Consider the Role of Afghan National Security Forces in Highway Security.** In the future, Afghan security forces will have a role to play in road security. Proposals to reform the convoy security scheme ought to take a medium- to long-term view of the role of Afghan security forces, while developing credible security alternatives that address the immediate U.S. military logistics needs.
4. **Inventory Actual Trucking Capacity Available to the Department of Defense.** The Department of Defense should conduct a survey of the available trucking capacity in Afghanistan under the HNT contract to ensure that its needs will be met with the additional forces under orders to deploy to Afghanistan.
5. **Draft Contracts to Ensure Transparency of Subcontractors.** Contracts between the Department of Defense and its trucking and/or security prime contractors need to include provisions that ensure a line of sight, and accountability, between the Department and the relevant subcontractors. Where Department of Defense regulations already require such provisions, the Department needs to enforce them.
6. **Oversee Contracts to Ensure Contract Transparency and Performance.** The Department of Defense needs to provide the personnel and resources required to manage and oversee its trucking and security contracts in Afghanistan. Contracts of this magnitude and of this consequence require travel 'outside the wire.' For convoys, that means having the force protection resources necessary for mobility of military logistics personnel to conduct periodic unannounced inspections and ride-alongs.
7. **Analyze Effect of Coalition Contracting on Afghan Corruption.** The national security components of the U.S. government, including

the Department of Defense, the Department of State, the U.S. Agency for International Development, the Department of Justice, and the intelligence community, need to systematically track and analyze the effects of U.S., NATO, and other international contracting on corruption in Afghanistan.

II. BACKGROUND

Supplying the Troops

Afghanistan ... is a landlocked country whose neighbors range from uneasy U.S. allies, such as Pakistan and Uzbekistan, to outright adversaries, such as Iran. Thirty years of war have devastated what little infrastructure the country had. In the south, scattered population centers are separated by deserts; in the east, they're divided by mountains. Winter brings storms and snow; spring brings floods.[2]

The U.S. operation in Afghanistan has presented the U.S. military with the most complex logistical operation it has ever undertaken. By September 2010, under President Barack Obama's plan to increase troop strength, the United States will have 100,000 troops in Afghanistan, with an additional 38,000 allied forces under NATO command. Military logistics officers are responsible for providing the troops with the food, water, shelter, weapons, ammunition, and fuel they need to perform their duties.

To put the scope of the logistics operation into perspective, U.S. and NATO forces required 1.1 million gallons of fuel *per day* in 2009. That year, as troop levels grew from 31,800 to 68,000, U.S. military and contractor planes delivered 187,394 tons of cargo.[3] Given that the backbone of the military's distribution network is overland, the cargo transported by trucks is nearly ten times that amount. Eighty percent of goods and materiel reach Afghanistan by land.[4]

Getting cargo to Afghanistan is a tricky endeavor. Unlike Iraq, which has access to the Persian Gulf and is bordered by several U.S. allies, Afghanistan is landlocked between countries with unstable security, impenetrable geographic barriers, and governments hostile to the United States. The most direct route to redeploy goods and materiel from Iraq to Afghanistan runs through Iran and is therefore unusable. To the north, the government in

Turkmenistan has refused to allow U.S. supply routes to pass through the country.

There are two main land routes into Afghanistan, one from the south through Pakistan and the other from the north through Central Asia. The southern route is the most used and the most dangerous. Cargo is processed in the port of Karachi and then sent north, where it must pass through "the Pashtun tribal lands, where insurgents unfriendly to both Kabul and Islamabad have strong support."[5] These insurgents include the Quetta Shura, led by the top leaders of the deposed Afghan Taliban. On June 8, 2010, for example, militants in Pakistan attacked a convoy of contractor supply trucks carrying U.S. goods as it stopped at a depot just outside of Islamabad, burning 30 trucks and killing six.[6]

The northern route through Central Asia is safer, but also longer and significantly more expensive, adding 10-20 days of transport time and two to three times the cost. The northern route also passes through several countries, necessitating significant diplomatic support to ensure that border crossings run smoothly.[7] Central Asia is also plagued by pockets of political instability. In Kyrgyzstan, for example, the sitting president was deposed in April. The country's southern region, which includes important rail networks used for U.S. supplies, has erupted in an ethnic pogrom.[8]

The fastest route to Afghanistan is by air. However, the lack of airport infrastructure places significant constraints on the military's ability to rely on air transport to supply the troops. Afghanistan has only 16 airports with paved runways, and of those, only four are accessible to non-military aircraft (including contractor-operated cargo planes).[9] Air transport is also the most costly shipping option. Thus, while air transport is available, it is limited to personnel and high-priority cargo. Only about 20 percent of cargo reaches Afghanistan by air.[10]

Distribution within Afghanistan

Once cargo reaches Afghanistan, it is taken to one of a handful of distribution hubs, the largest of which are Bagram Airfield in the north and Kandahar Airfield in the south. From there, the supplies must be distributed throughout the country to over 200 U.S. forward operating bases and combat outposts, many of which are located in remote and dangerous areas. While helicopters can be used for some transport, harsh flying conditions, weight limits, frequent maintenance downtimes, high costs, and the sheer size of the country place significant limits on how much helicopters can be utilized.[11] Thus, the vast majority of in-country transport is accomplished by truck.

Afghanistan presents a uniquely challenging environment for ground transport. The terrain is unforgiving: deserts that kick up sandstorms in the summer become flooded and muddy in the spring, and treacherous mountain roads leave no room for error. Summer heat regularly reaches 120 degrees. Mountain weather can change in an instant, bringing snow and freezing rain. In the winter, the single tunnel that connects Kabul to northern Afghanistan is frequently cut off by avalanches. A break-down in the mountains can close a route for days, until the vehicle can be disassembled and airlifted out.[12] The lack of infrastructure – including a dearth of paved roads – leaves drivers to face the elements unassisted.

If terrain and weather were not challenging enough, man-made hazards pose an even bigger threat to trucks in Afghanistan. Explosives can be easily planted and concealed along transport routes, and insurgents regularly attack. General Duncan McNabb, commander of U.S. Transportation Command, told Congress last year, "[i]f you ask me what I worry about at night, it is the fact that our supply chain is always under attack."[13]

Finally, limited processing capacity at the distribution hubs can delay distribution. For example, Kandahar Airfield has had significant problems handling the volume of cargo it receives, leading to backlogs of trucks waiting to take goods for distribution. A 24-hour truck yard for trucks contracted to carry military supplies has alleviated the problem to some degree, but delays persist.[14] Contractors report that in some instances their drivers have waited outside Kandahar Airfield for several weeks until they were permitted to unload cargo.

Taken together, these elements pose considerable challenges for the logistics officers in charge of making sure supplies reach the troops. The experience of the U.S. military in Iraq a country with decent infrastructure and manageable terrain-is not comparable. As a senior military official who has spent time in both Iraq and Afghanistan noted, "[i] n Iraq, logistics was on cruise control. In Afghanistan, it's graduate-level logistics to make it happen."[15] Another official described Afghanistan as "the harshest logistics environment on earth."[16]

"In Iraq, logistics was on cruise control. In Afghanistan, it's graduate-level logistics to make it happen."

- Senior U.S. Military Official

Despite the best efforts of military logisticians, the supply chain does not always work, delaying critical life support to the troops. A military official who served in Afghanistan in 2007 and 2008 noted that at times "we had guys out there at the outposts in my area of operations starving because we couldn't get resupply in to them."[17]

Afghan Trucking

The U.S. military relies on local Afghan trucking companies for almost all of its ground transport needs. The trucking industry is a key part of the Afghan economy, providing employment opportunities for a large segment of the population who otherwise would have trouble finding work due to the high rate of illiteracy. U.S. trucking contracts provide a relatively lucrative source of income in this very poor country. The owner of one of the trucking companies supporting the U.S. supply chain reported that between the drivers, assistant drivers, managers, and mechanics, his company single-handedly feeds 20,000 people.[18]

According to this owner, "truck drivers are captains of their own ships."[19] With little infrastructure to support them, a driver and his assistant (usually a young son) must have the wherewithal to survive for weeks or even months on the road. Truckers will often decorate their trucks in an ornate manner, and these so-called "Jingle Trucks" – named for the sound they make as they drive – are found throughout the roads of Afghanistan.

The Host Nation Trucking Contract

The HNT contract is a $2.16 billion dollar indefinite delivery/indefinite quantity (IDIQ) contract to provide ground transportation in Afghanistan for over 70 percent of Department of Defense goods and materiel, including food, water, fuel, equipment, and ammunition.[20] The Department of Defense initially requested a statement of capabilities for the current HNT contract in August 2008 and issued a request for proposals in September 2008. Thirty-five contractors submitted bids, and the competitive range was narrowed to ten.[21]

Source: GAO analysis of data from the Consultative Group for the Transport Sector and USAID.

Supplemented by Subcommittee staff

Photo Credit: Defense Imagery

The contract was awarded to six contractors on March 15, 2009, and performance began on May 1, 2009.[22] Although the contract started with a total contract cap of $360 million dollars, according to the Department of Defense, "[t]wo weeks after performance began requirements skyrocketed at a pace that acquisition planners could not have anticipated" due to the surge in troops.[23] In July 2009, Acting Assistant Secretary of the Army Dean Popps signed a "Justification and Approval for Out of Scope Modification" that increased the total contract size to $2.16 billion, with an individual cap of $360 million per HNT contractor.[24] For context, the total annual gross domestic product of Afghanistan was just over $13 billion in 2009.[25]

Prior to this HNT contract, the Department of Defense's supply transportation was provided under a blanket purchase agreement (BPA)[26] with several companies, some of whom are now prime or sub-contractors for the current HNT contract. The new HNT contract was conceived to add capacity, simplify pricing, and solve several problems with the BPA, including concerns regarding corruption and bribery among BPA contractors and, in one case, a U.S. Army contracting officer.[27]

The "Contractor is Responsible for All Security"

Importantly, the HNT contract included one new critical provision: section 4.9 of the Statement of Work provides that the "Contractor is responsible for all security" and that "[t] he Contractor will conduct convoys independently, without military escorts, unless otherwise determined by the USG [U.S. government] at its sole direction." The Statement of Work acknowledges the risk to drivers: "the USG will not intentionally direct the Contractor to pass through an area where the chance of hostilities is high. However, the USG cannot foreclose the possibility of hostile acts occurring."[28]

The Statement of Work further regulates the minimum security that each HNT contractor must provide for each mission: two security vehicles for every five trucks. In addition, the contract provides that "all weapons utilized will be provided by the Contractor and will be within the prescribed USG authorized weapon listing."[29]

Department of Defense Management and Oversight of HNT

Operational management of the HNT contract was initially handled by the 484th Movement Control Battalion of the U.S. Army.[30] In February 2010, the 419th Movement Control Battalion took over management of the contract.[31] For HNT, both movement control battalions reported to the 143rd Expeditionary Sustainment Brigade.

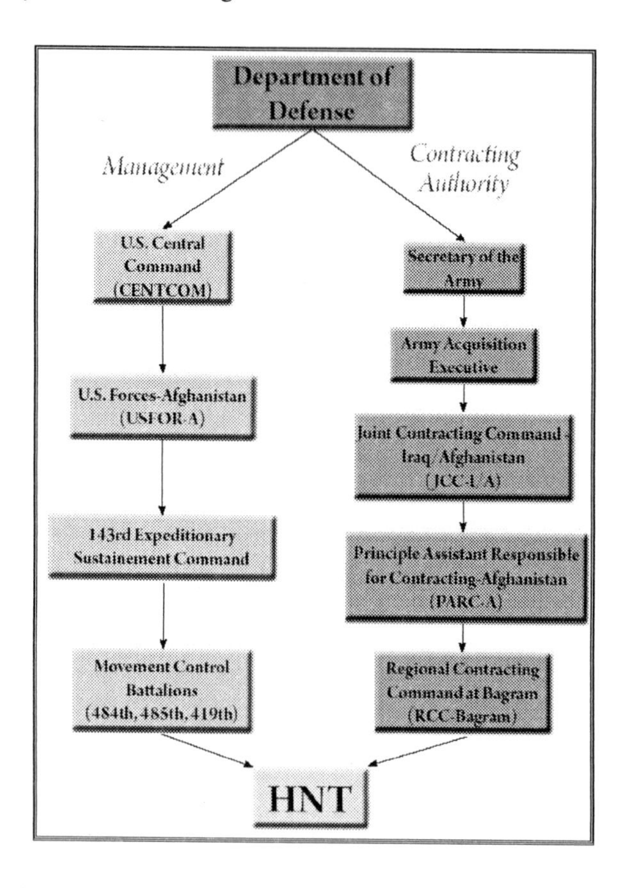

Actual signing authority for the HNT contract flowed through a complex hierarchy of military commands. The HNT contract is immediately overseen by the Regional Contracting Center in Bagram (RCC-Bagram). RCC-Bagram is one of a handful of contracting centers in Afghanistan that report to the Principal Assistant Responsible for Contracting-Afghanistan (PARC-A). The PARC-A reports to the Joint Contracting Command-Iraq/Afghanistan (JCC-I/A). JCC-I/A gets contracting authority from the Army Acquisition Executive and the Secretary of the Army, but as a practical matter reports to the Commander of U.S. Central Command (CENTCOM).

> ***"The Contractor is responsible for all security. The Contractor will conduct convoys independently, without military escorts, unless otherwise destermined by the U.S. government at its sole discretion."***
>
> *- HNT Statement of Work*

HNT Contractors

The HNT contract was originally awarded to six contractors, four of whom previously held contracts under the BPA. In late 2009, two additional companies were added, both of which had previous trucking experience under the BPA.[32] The two companies that had not been prime contractors under the BPA had both worked as subcontractors under that agreement.

Several of the prime contractors for HNT do not own trucks and subcontract out all of their trucking needs. In other words, they essentially serve as brokers to the local Afghan trucking companies. In several cases, the prime contractors have only a handful of personnel in Afghanistan, and in at least one case, the contractor had no prior experience in the trucking business. Prime contractors reported that there is a finite "pool" of trucks in Afghanistan, and many of the prime contractors compete with each other through subcontractors for the use of the same vehicles.[33]

The following companies are prime contractors under the HNT contract:[34]

NCL Holdings (N CL) – NCL was founded in May 2005 by Hamed Wardak, the son of the Afghan Defense Minister, Abdul Rahim Wardak. The company is based in Northern Virginia. Prior to receiving the HNT contract in 2009, NCL performed security operations in Afghanistan for Department of Defense contractors. NCL subcontracts out all of its trucking operations under HNT, and had no direct experience with managing trucking before this contract.

The Sandi Group – The Sandi Group is based in Washington, D.C. and has worked in private sector development in both Iraq and Afghanistan. To perform HNT missions, the Sandi Group has subcontracted out all trucking to local Afghan subcontractors.

Mesopotamia Group and EMA, Joint Venture – Mesopotamia Group, a Delaware- based company and EMA, an Afghan company, received an HNT contract as a joint venture after having worked on the BPA contract in a contractor-subcontractor relationship, with EMA as the local subcontractor. EMA owns many of its own trucks and also brokers with owner-operators from local tribes. Mesopotamia Group provides management and capital to the joint venture.

HEB International Logistics – HEB is an international logistics and transportation company based in Dubai. HEB owns some of its own trucks but principally relies on local Afghan subcontractors. HEB performed trucking operations under the BPA prior to receiving the HNT contract.

Anham, LLC – Anham is a partnership that was formed in 2004 by a Virginia-based investment group (HII-Finance), a Saudi conglomerate, and a Jordanian investment group. It is based in Dubai. Anham owns its own trucks and does not subcontract to local companies, but it performs far fewer missions than the leading HNT contractors.

The Four Horsemen International (Four Horsemen) **and Three Bullets Incorporated** (Three Bullets), **Joint Venture** – Four Horsemen is a New Jersey-based security company with principal operations in Afghanistan managed by Western military expatriates; Three Bullets is an Afghan-based transportation company that owns some of its own trucks and brokers with local owner-operators. Four Horsemen provides the security force for the joint venture. Four Horsemen had previously performed security operations under the BPA with other companies, and Three Bullets performed trucking operations on the BPA.

Afghan American Army Services (AAA) – AAA is Afghan-owned and was added to the HNT contract in November 2009 following a bid protest before the U.S. Government Accountability Office. AAA had previously worked under the BPA and had performed trucking operations since July 2006. Under HNT, AAA subcontracts out trucking operations to several local companies.

Guzar Mir Bacha Kot Transportation (GMT) – GMT is an Afghan-owned company that was added to the HNT contract in November 2009 in order to increase trucking capacity. GMT was a prime contractor on the BPA and the company has provided trucking services in Afghanistan for more than 15 years. GMT provides its own trucks and, before receiving the HNT contract, worked as a subcontractor for other HNT prime contractors.

The Afghan Security Environment

The security environment in Afghanistan has rapidly deteriorated in the past two years and, as a result, trucking operations have become increasingly dangerous.[35] The number of incidents involving trucks on the road, including ambushes, IEDs, and kidnappings, has risen sharply. Trucking companies also face repercussions for working with the U.S. military. One company owner reported that he and his drivers receive death threats for working with the United States and that he often has had to pay money to militants to recover the bodies of drivers who were killed on the roads.[36] Trucking convoys have become favorite targets of the Taliban and other insurgents, who frequently stop convoys to demand money, set the trucks on fire, and kill or kidnap the drivers.[37]

As the security situation has deteriorated, there has been a marked increase in the use of IEDs on Afghanistan's roads.[38] By one account, "all told, the U.S. military recorded 8,159 IED incidents in Afghanistan in 2009, compared with 3,867 in 2008 and 2,677 the year before."[39]

Lieutenant General Michael Oates, the director of the Department of Defense's Joint IED Defeat Organization, was quoted in March 2010: "[we] don't have years to wait and start changing the momentum in Afghanistan."[40] To add to the sense of urgency, a June 2010 *New York Times* article cited a U.N. report as finding that there has been "a near-doubling of roadside bombings for the first four months of 2010 compared with the same period in 2009."[41]

Private Security Contractors

According to the Afghan Ministry of Interior, there are currently 52 licensed private security companies with a total of roughly 25,000 registered armed guards in Afghanistan.[42] There are also hundreds of additional unregistered private security providers and some estimate up to 70,000 total private armed guards.[43] Given perilous security conditions in Afghanistan, U.S. and allied contractors in Afghanistan have little choice but to employ private security companies. Whether securing truck convoys, guarding a road project, or providing personal security details, private security services are widely used.

The U.S. military increasingly relies on private security contractors in Afghanistan for a variety of significant security needs, from transportation to static protection of U.S. bases.[44] Unlike in Iraq where a majority of the armed guards are third-country nationals (*e.g.*, Peruvians, Ugandans, Nepalese), 95 percent of the private armed guards used by the Department of Defense in Afghanistan are local nationals. Indeed, the Department's "Afghan First" campaign directs contractors to hire at least half of all workers from nearby towns or villages.[45]

Department of Defense Private Security Contractor Personnel[46]	**Total**	**U.S. Citizens**	**Third Country National**	**Local/Host Country National**
Afghanistan	14,439	114	409	13,916
Iraq	11,095	776	9,127	1,192

Regulation of Private Security Contractors

There are significant legal and regulatory restrictions on the use of private security contractors. Although Department of Defense regulations provide that it should only use private security contractors licensed with the host nation, the military directly employs a significant number of unlicensed private security contractors for use as guards at its forward operating bases.[47]

Notably, in a 2006 memorandum on the legality of using private security contractors to protect U.S. personnel and property in Iraq, a Department of Defense Deputy General Counsel wrote:

> [T]his opinion should not be construed to mean that contractors may perform all security functions in Iraq and Afghanistan. Private Security Companies should not be employed in situations where the likelihood of direct participation in hostilities is high. For example, they should not be employed in quick-reaction force (QRF) missions, local patrolling, or military convoy security operations where the likelihood of hostile contact is high.[48]

The Department of Defense's use of private security contractors in Iraq and Afghanistan has received significant media attention over the last several years. High-profile incidents in which security contractors were accused of shooting civilians, using excessive force, being insensitive to local customs or beliefs, or otherwise behaving inappropriately prompted Congress to call for regulations to increase oversight and accountability of private security contractorss employed in contingency operations.

In July 2009, the Department promulgated Instruction 3020.50, *Private Security Contractors Operating in Contingency Operations*, which established policies for selecting, training, equipping, and managing private security contractors in contingency operations. This regulation, which was mandated under the National Defense Authorization Act of Fiscal Year 2008,[49] requires the Department of Defense to account for private security contractor equipment, track incidents involving their personnel, and investigate any of the following occurrences:

1. The injury or death of private security contractor personnel;
2. The discharge of weapons by or at such personnel;
3. The injury, death, or damage of property caused by the actions of such personnel; or
4. Incidents of alleged misconduct.

The regulations make clear that they also apply to private security contractor subcontractors working for Department of Defense contractors.[50]

III. Findings

1. Security for the U.S. Supply Chain Is Principally Provided by Warlords

Finding: The principal private security subcontractors on the HNT contract are warlords, strongmen, commanders, and militia leaders who compete with the Afghan central government for power and authority. Providing "protection" services for the U.S. supply chain empowers these warlords with money, legitimacy, and a *raison d'etre* for their private armies. Although many of these warlords nominally operate under private security companies licensed by the Afghan Ministry of Interior, the warlords thrive in a vacuum of government authority and their interests are in fundamental conflict with U.S. aims to build a strong Afghan government.

Commander Ruhullah is prototypical of a new class of warlord in Afghanistan. He commands a small army of over 600 armed guards. His men engage in regular combat with insurgent forces. He claims extraordinary casualty figures on both sides (450 of his own men killed in the last year and many more Taliban dead). He readily admits to bribing governors, police chiefs, and army generals. Over a cup of tea in Dubai, he complained to the Subcommittee staff about the high cost of ammunition in Afghanistan – he says he spends $1.5 million *per month* on rounds for an arsenal that includes AK-47s, heavy machine guns, and RPGs.[51] Villagers along the road refer to him as "the Butcher."[52]

Commander Ruhullah is largely a mystery to both the U.S. government and the contractors that employ his services.

Before September 11, 2001, Commander Ruhullah was relatively unknown in Afghanistan. Today, he is the single largest security provider for the U.S. supply chain in Afghanistan. Despite this critical and sensitive role, nobody from the Department of Defense or the U.S. intelligence community has ever met with him (except for a brief detention by U.S. Special Forces on what he says are false drug charges). Commander Ruhullah is largely a mystery to both the U.S. government and the contractors that employ his services. Indeed, several of the prime HNT contractors are apparently unaware that Commander Ruhullah guards their trucks (their security subcontractors utilize his services without the prime contractors' knowledge).

Commander Ruhullah dominates the private security business along Highway 1, the main transportation artery between Kabul and Kandahar. Because most U.S. supplies are shippd through Pakistan to Bagram Airfield, north of Kabul, while most U.S. troops are surging into Kandahar, in the south, Highway 1 is the critical route for the supply chain within Afghanistan.

No private security companies working for the United States are supposed to useany weapon more high-powered than an AK-47. Commander Ruhullah's men use heavy machine guns and rocket-propelled grenades.

Commander Ruhullah says that he guards roughly 3,500 U.S. supply trucks every month. The prime contractors and local Afghan subcontractors that use his services pay him and the security company that he associates with, Watan Risk Management, handsomely. For security between Maydan Shahr (just south of Kabul) and Kandahar, Commander Ruhullah charges up to $1,500 per truck.[53]

At the behest of Congress, the Department of Defense has promulgated extensive regulations intended to improve oversight and accountability of private security contractors in contingency operations such as Iraq and

Afghanistan. Commander Ruhullah has never heard of the regulations and says that they do not apply to him. No private security companies working for the United States are supposed to use any weapon more high-powered than an AK-47. Commander Ruhullah's men use heavy machine guns and RPGs.[54]

Commander Ruhullah is just one of dozens of warlords, strongmen, and commanders who have found a niche in providing security services to the U.S. military in Afghanistan. Some are well-known tribal leaders or former mujahedeen who have been in the business of war for the past thirty years. Others, like Commander Ruhullah, are relative newcomers whose power and influence are directly derivative of their contracting and subcontracting work for the U.S. government.

Both the old and new warlords' interests are in fundamental conflict with a properly functioning government. By definition, warlords wield military might and violence outside of the theoretical government monopoly on those tools. Warlordism is antithetical to the Afghan state, and ultimately to U.S. counterinsurgency strategy in Afghanistan, yet these warlords have flourished providing security for the U.S. supply chain there.

Warlordism in Afghanistan

Not all warlords are created equal. At the top of the hierarchy are the well-known tribal leaders, former mujahedeen commanders, or local power brokers who command the loyalty of men beyond their ability to provide a paycheck. For these warlords, providing security to U.S. and NATO convoys is just the latest iteration of long and colorful careers in war-torn Afghanistan. Long after the United States leaves Afghanistan, and the convoy security business shuts down, these warlords will likely continue to play a major role as autonomous centers of political, economic, and military power.[55]

Other warlords are newer to the scene but have grown in strength based on their ability to feed off U.S. and NATO security contracting, particularly the highly lucrative business niche of providing private security for the coalition supply chain. Men serve and die for these warlords for money, not tribal, ethnic, or political loyalty. In Afghan culture, this new class of warlord is undeserving of that elevated title because their power is derivative of their business function, not their political or tribal clout.[56]

Watan Risk Management Toyota Hi-Lux security truck equipped with a .50 caliber anti-aircraft DSHK machine gun Photo Credit: Defense Imagery

According to one expert on Afghanistan, "the partial conversion of Afghan warlords into businessmen resembles in many ways the establishment of mafia networks, which are active both in the legal and the illegal economy and are able to use force to protect their interests and possibly to expand."[57] Whether called "businessmen," "commanders," "strongmen," "militia leaders," or "warlords," any single individual who commands hundreds or thousands of armed men in regular combat and operates largely outside the direct control of the central government is a competitor to the legitimacy of the state.[58]

Private Security Companies

Both President Karzai and the American-led coalition have made the disarmament of "illegal armed groups" (warlords, commanders, and militias) a top priority for success in Afghanistan. Since 2003, however, the disarmament, demobilization, and reintegration program has largely failed. Rather than disarm, many of the warlords and militia groups evaded the program by becoming private security companies for the coalition. According to an academic text on disarmament, "[c] ommanders thus appear to be using PSCs [private security companies] and other government security forces to hide their militias... [A] commander's strength is expressed less in terms of offensive capability against an opposing unit than in terms of the ability to acquire supporting contracts, to maintain armed units and to integrate into official and quasiofficial security structures."[59]

> ***"Warlords in Kandahar had been allowed to build up militias that they claimed were private security companies, and these private security companies were a creation of the international community."***
>
> *– UK Major General Nick Carter*

Major General Nick Carter, the British head of NATO's Regional Command-South in Kandahar, told reporters that "warlords in Kandahar had been allowed to build up militias that they claimed were private security companies," and that these private security companies were "a creation of the international community."[60] Ahmed Wali Karzai, President Hamid Karzai's brother, agrees: "[the guards] are the ones who know how to make bombs and shoot AK-47s. They are well-experienced jihadi foot soldiers. Most of them are now part of security companies." If they were not working for the security companies, Mr. Karzai stated, they would likely join the Taliban.[61]

Warlords Control the Highways

A warlord's power is principally derived from his ability to control security within a defined territory. The business of warlordism is to seek rents from those who would occupy that space, whether the local population or trucks attempting to transit through it. Given the extremely limited road network in Afghanistan, highways are prime real estate. If a highway also happens to be a critical component of the U.S. supply chain for the distribution of goods in Afghanistan, the opportunity for rent-seeking is massive. Of course, the business model depends on the warlord's ability to monopolize control of the highway and to fight off competition.

In Afghanistan, warlords control many of the main highways used by the U.S. supply chain, particularly in the south, east, and west. Sophisticated consumers of the Afghan road network (the local Afghan trucking companies) have learned how to navigate this patchwork of highway warlords by paying the right warlord at the right section of highway. Like a *prix fixe* menu, a list provided to the Subcommittee by an HNT contractor details which "escort provider" operates on which sections of road between various U.S. forward operating bases in Afghanistan:[62]

#	Origin	Destination	the escort provider	COMPANY NAME
1	AIR BORNE	SAYED BAD	COMMANDER ROHULLAH	WATAN RISK MANAGEMENT
2	AIR BORNE	CARWILE	COMMANDER ROHULLAH	WATAN RISK MANAGEMENT
3	AIR BORNE	GHAZNI	COMMANDER ROHULLAH	WATAN RISK MANAGEMENT
4	AIR BORNE	FOUR CORNERS	COMMANDER ROHULLAH	WATAN RISK MANAGEMENT
5	AIR BORNE	SHARANA	COMMANDER ROHULLAH	WATAN RISK MANAGEMENT
6	AIR BORNE	WARRIOR	COMMANDER ROHULLAH	WATAN RISK MANAGEMENT
7	AIR BORNE	APPACHE	COMMANDER ROHULLAH	WATAN RISK MANAGEMENT
8	AIR BORNE	KANDAHAR	COMMANDER ROHULLAH	WATAN RISK MANAGEMENT
9	AIR BORNE	LASHKARGHA	COMMANDER ROHULLAH	WATAN RISK MANAGEMENT
10	AIR BORNE	BASTION	COMMANDER ROHULLAH	WATAN RISK MANAGEMENT
11	AIR BORNE	LEATHERNICK	COMMANDER ROHULLAH	WATAN RISK MANAGEMENT
12	AIR BORNE	FARAH	COMMANDER ROHULLAH	WATAN RISK MANAGEMENT
13	AIR BORNE	SHINDAND	COMMANDER ROHULLAH	WATAN RISK MANAGEMENT
14	AIR BORNE	HEART	COMMANDER ROHULLAH	WATAN RISK MANAGEMENT
15	AIR BORNE	QALA E NOW	COMMANDER ROHULLAH	WATAN RISK MANAGEMENT
16	AIR BORNE	TRAIN KWOT	COMMANDER ROHULLAH	WATAN RISK MANAGEMENT
17	AIR BORNE	FRONTENACK	COMMANDER ROHULLAH	WATAN RISK MANAGEMENT
18	AIR BORNE	LUNDELL	COMMANDER ROHULLAH	WATAN RISK MANAGEMENT
19	AIR BORNE	DERAWOOD	COMMANDER ROHULLAH	WATAN RISK MANAGEMENT
20	GHAZNI	SHARANA	COMMANDER RAHIM	NO COMPANY
21	GHAZNI	FOUR CORNERS	COMMANDER RAHIM	NO COMPANY
22	QALAT	WOLVRINE	ANA	NO COMPANY
23	QALAT	SWEENY	ANA	NO COMPANY
24	KANDAHAR	SPIN BOLDAK	ANP	NO COMPANY
25	KANDAHAR	FRONTENACK	COMMANDER MATIULLAH	NO COMPANY
26	KANDAHAR	TRAIN KWOT	COMMANDER MATIULLAH	NO COMPANY
27	KANDAHAR	LUNDELL	COMMANDER MATIULLAH	NO COMPANY
28	KANDAHAR	DERAWOOD	COMMANDER MATIULLAH	NO COMPANY
29	KANDAHAR	QALAT	COMMANDER MASUD	NO COMPANY
30	KANDAHAR	WOLVRINE	COMMANDER MASUD	NO COMPANY
31	KANDAHAR	SWEENY	COMMANDER MASUD	NO COMPANY
32	KANDAHAR	BULLARD	COMMANDER MASUD	NO COMPANY
33	KANDAHAR	LASHKARGHA	COMMANDER ANGAR	NO COMPANY
34	KANDAHAR	BASTION	RAHMAT	NO COMPANY
35	KANDAHAR	LEATHERNICK	MASUD	NO COMPANY
36	KANDAHAR	RAMROD	MASUD	NO COMPANY
37	KANDAHAR	MAIWAND	MASUD	NO COMPANY
38	KANDAHAR	DWYER	KAKA SHARB	NO COMPANY
39	KANDAHAR	DWYER	TURIAN	NO COMPANY
40	KANDAHAR	DWYER	KOKA	NO COMPANY
41	KANDAHAR	DELARM	COMMANDER HABIBULLAH	NO COMPANY
42	KANDAHAR	SHINDAND	COMMANDER HABIBULLAH	NO COMPANY
43	KANDAHAR	STONE	COMMANDER HABIBULLAH	NO COMPANY
44	KANDAHAR	FARAH	COMMANDER HABIBULLAH	NO COMPANY

Commander Ruhullah and Watan Risk Management

Commander Ruhullah dominates the critical section of Highway 1 between Kabul and Kandahar, an area that is the central supply artery for the U.S. and NATO mission in southern Afghanistan and also happens to be heavily infiltrated by the Taliban.[63]

The U.S. supply chain operates on Ruhullah's schedule; his local sub-commanders will wait several days to gather as many trucks as possible before moving, even if sometrucks are days or weeks overdue at their destinations.

In a typical convoy movement, Commander Ruhullah assembles between 200-400 trucks carrying U.S. supplies in Maydan Shahr, just south of Kabul. The U.S. supply chain operates on his schedule; his local sub-commanders will wait several days to gather as many trucks as possible before moving, even if some trucks are days or weeks overdue at their destination. Commander Ruhullah guards the convoy with teams of several hundred men. The guards travel in pickup trucks and SUVs. Some trucks have mounted heavy machine guns and many others carry RPGs. The trip takes roughly three days and a different team handles each leg.[64]

Commander Ruhullah operates under the license of Watan Risk Management, a registered security company owned by Ahmed Rateb Popal and Rashid Popal, two cousins of President Karzai. Watan Risk Management has some Western management, a website, and contracts to protect U.S. forward operating bases and U.S.-funded development projects. The Popals welcomed an interview with the Subcommittee staff and spoke candidly about their operations. Commander Ruhullah runs convoy security operations with relative autonomy; the Popals provide some Western interface (they speak perfect English) and their company's security license. The Popal brothers are eager to exit the convoy security business due to the headache of recent negative publicity.[65]

Whether they know it or not, most of the HNT prime contractors use Commander Ruhullah for security. Of the eight prime HNT contractors, all but one contract directly or indirectly with Watan Risk Management.

Whether they know it or not, most of the HNT prime contractors use Commander Ruhullah for security. Of the eight prime HNT contractors, all but one contract directly or indirectly with Watan Risk Management. Only a very small handful of convoy security providers travel that section of Highway 1 without employing Commander Ruhullah's services.[66] Those competitors and the trucks that they protect claim to experience abnormally high incident rates.[67]

Photo Credit: Subcommittee Staff

At a price of up to $1,500 per truck, and with several thousand HNT trucks traveling between Kabul and Kandahar every month, Commander Ruhullah and Watan Risk Management make several tens of millions of dollars per year providing convoy security.[68]

Kandahar Security Force

With the Popal brothers eager to leave the convoy security business, Commander Ruhullah has new aspirations: establishing a single brokerage firm that will serve to connect coalition contractors to most of the principal local warlords in their respective regions within southern Afghanistan. The "Kandahar Security Force," as it will be called, will include two dozen warlords and commanders who have been providing unregistered private security services in and around Kandahar. Commander Ruhullah will be president of this new venture.[69]

Commander Ruhullah explained that the reason for creating the Kandahar Security Force was to "legitimize" the security providers that are already operating in the region. These security providers will operate under the Kandahar Security Force flag, but each will be given his own separate contracts and Commander Ruhullah believes there will be no internal competition.[70] Ahmed Rateb Popal of Watan Risk Management believes that the Kandahar Security Force simply gives the gloss of an official license to a collection of warlords and commanders. He wants a "clean government," but said that the current government is "too weak," and transporters have "no choice" but to rely on these warlords and commanders. His brother, Rashid Popal, agreed and stated that the current situation "creates a state of anarchy."

In his view, the Kandahar Security Force "will not improve the security situation."[71]

In sum, Commander Ruhullah hopes to create a confederation that would monopolize private security in and around Kandahar just as Kandahar is becoming the key strategic focal point of the U.S. mission. His proposal for a license for the Kandahar Security Force is pending before the Afghan cabinet's security committee.[72]

Operating under the façade of a registered private security company will bring the unlicensed warlords who join Kandahar Security Force into technical compliance with Afghan licensing requirements but it will not fundamentally change the way they operate or improve their accountability. When asked what kind of oversight and control he would have over the collection of commanders that he would lead, Commander Ruhullah stated simply that, in the event of any problems, he would "take care of it."[73]

If approved, the Kandahar Security Force would become the single largest private security provider in Afghanistan. According to Commander Ruhullah and the Popals, the idea to create the Kandahar Security Force originated with former Afghan Interior Minister Hanif Atmar, and has been approved by the Ministry of Interior's anti-terrorism department.[74] Some top Afghan officials have supported the proposal, ostensibly as a means of uniting and controlling powerful, unregistered groups that they depict as competing violently for coalition contracts.[75]

Others have raised concerns that the consolidation of private security commanders in southern Afghanistan will further empower Ahmed Wali Karzai, the powerful head of the Kandahar Provincial Council and the brother of President Karzai. Carl Forsberg of the Institute for the Study of War describes Ahmed Wali Karzai's *modus operandi* as gaining "the loyalty of militia commanders in exchange for distributing lucrative contracts from international actors."[76] Mr. Forsberg adds, "Ahmed Wali Karzai's connections and influence allow him to collect a cut of most of the business transactions occurring in Kandahar City."[77]

In an interview with the Subcommittee staff, Ahmed Wali Karzai denied any operational or beneficial involvement in the Kandahar Security Force. He said that he has never been involved with any private security company and that he only helped to facilitate the meeting in which the individual commanders had agreed to come together under a "single umbrella." Mr. Karzai believes that the creation of the Kandahar Security Force will be beneficial because it will allow unregistered commanders to register their guards, vehicles, and weapons. He said that the commanders had also been asked to limit their movements within Kandahar City and to transfer their bases of operation to outside the city.[78] Commander Ruhullah was similarly adamant that Ahmed Wali Karzai was not "involved in any way" with the creation of the Kandahar Security Force: "He will have no ownership whatsoever."[79]

In any event, if the Kandahar Security Force does come to fruition, it will undoubtedly take over from Watan Risk Management as the principal private security provider and broker for the U.S. supply chain in Afghanistan.

Commander Matiullah Khan

Matiullah Khan is the leading private security provider and principal warlord of Uruzgan Province, just north of Kandahar. Matiullah's nominal title is chief of the provincial highway police, despite the fact that the highway police force was disbanded years ago. He commands an armed militia of over 2,000 men, called the Kandak Amniante Uruzgan (KAU), and controls all traffic along the main highway between Kandahar and Tarin Kowt, the provincial Uruzgan capital.[80]

In a recent front page profile, the *New York Times* described Matiullah as the "most powerful man" in Uruzgan:

> Matiullah Khan [is] the head of a private army that earns millions of dollars guarding NATO supply convoys... In little more than two years, Mr. Matiullah, an illiterate former highway patrol commander, has grown stronger than the government of Oruzgan Province, not only supplanting its role in providing security but usurping its other functions, his rivals say, like appointing public employees and doling out government largess. His fighters run missions with American Special Forces, and when Afghan officials have confronted him, he has either rebuffed them or had them removed.[81]

Ahmed Wali Karzai credits Matiullah with almost single-handedly making Uruzgan Province safe. He describes him as a "very successful police officer" who is "in charge of highway patrol" and earned the support of the people. He claims that "the Taliban have been defeated in Uruzgan," largely because of Matiullah. According to Mr. Karzai, Matiullah also uses his armed force, the KAU, to fight Taliban in neighboring provinces, including Northern Kandahar and Zabol.[82]

Every HNT contractor and subcontractor assigned to take U.S. supplies to Uruzgan exclusively uses Matiullah's security services at a cost of between $1,500 and $3,000 per truck, per mission. The CEO of a private security company in Afghanistan stated that, "Matiullah has the road from Kandahar to Tarin Kowt completely under his control. No one can travel without Matiullah without facing consequences. There is no other way to get there. You have to either pay him or fight him."[83]

Private trucking companies supporting the Dutch and Australian forces based in Uruzgan also exclusively use Matiullah for highway security.[84] With over 200 support trucks per month for these NATO forces, news accounts estimated that he earned $4 million to $6 million per year from NATO security alone.[85]

Matiullah is the nephew of Jan Mohammad Khan, the deposed governor of Uruzgan. When the Dutch took responsibility for Uruzgan in 2006, they demanded that President Karzai fire Jan Mohammad Khan for his notorious drug smuggling and human rights abuses. Subsequently, the Dutc blocked Matiullah from being formally named as the police chief because of his human rights record as his uncle's leading enforcer.[86] According to press accounts, "[h] e led the hit squads that killed stubborn farmers who did not want to surrender their land, daughters, and livestock to the former governor."[87] One high-ranking Dutch official claimed that Matiullah is so feared that, "[i]f we appoint Matiullah police chief, probably more than half of all people in the Baluchi valley would run over to the Taliban immediately."[88]

> ***"Matiullah has the road from Kandahar to Tarin Kowt completely under his control. You have to either pay him or fight him."***
>
> – Private Security Company Executive

Although the NATO forces stationed in Uruzgan are totally dependent on Matiullah to permit their supply convoys to travel the roads he controls, they publicly distance themselves from him. In response to press inquiries, a Dutch government spokesman stated that the Dutch Ministry of Defense does not pay Matiullah directly, but "it is up to local transporters whether they find it necessary to pay for protection."[89] Meanwhile, "[t] he [Australian Defense Forces] will neither confirm nor deny knowledge of payments to Colonel Khan," but privately they acknowledged to reporters that they are dependent upon his permission for their supply routes.[90]

Colonel Abdul Razziq

Abdul Razziq has many titles – "Commander," "Colonel," "General," "Director" – but what matters is that he controls the Chaman-Spin Boldak border crossing, the crucial gateway for all supplies coming from Pakistan directly to southern Afghanistan. At age 30, Colonel Razziq is the chief of the Achakzai tribe which straddles the border area. His semi-official title is the chief of staff of the provincial border police. "According to U.S. military officials, Razziq wields near total control over Spin Boldak and the border crossing... [He] owns a trucking company, commands 3,500 police, effectively controls the local government, and reportedly takes in millions from extorting passing vehicles and trafficking drugs."[91]

During a congressional delegation to Afghanistan, U.S. and NATO commanders readily acknowledged that Colonel Razziq takes a major cut of all trucking that passes through the "Friendship Gate" at the border crossing, but they believe they are so dependent on his tight grip over the border they have no choice but to work with him.[92] Indeed, in mid-January 2010, General Stanley McChrystal himself flew to Spin Boldak to encourage Colonel Razziq to increase traffic and improve efficiency along the border.[93]

It is not clear how much Colonel Razziq earns from taxing U.S. and NATO supply convoys crossing the border, but, according to one former high-level member of his border police, he makes between $5 million and $6 million per month from his various border businesses.[94]

Pacha Khan Zadran

Pacha Khan Zadran, also known as "the Iron Grandpa," is currently a member of the Upper Parliament in Afghanistan, owns significant trucking assets, and provides convoy security in and around Paktia and Khost provinces.[95] He is a former mujahedeen who helped to topple the Taliban regime in 2001. He was appointed governor of Paktia Province by Hamid Karzai in December 2001, but was forced out of office in February 2002.[96] He responded violently, "many lives were lost as his fighters rocketed Gardez from the surrounding hills."[97] He was arrested by Pakistan in 2003 over "renegade" activities, including attacking government forces in Paktia, though he was allowed to return to Afghanistan in 2004.[98] Pacha Khan reportedly commands a private militia of 2,000 men who "control all major checkpoints on the main roads." But, Pacha Khan objects to the term "warlord": "They must not call us warlords. If you call us warlords, we will kill you."[99]

According to the *Boston Globe*, "[a]t least five people were held for years at Guantanamo Bay prison partly because they allegedly had ties to Pacha Khan Zadran."[100] Pacha Khan himself was never imprisoned there and was pardoned by President Karzai following his return to Afghanistan in 2004.[101] He became a member of Parliament in 2005.[102]

Pacha Khan and his three sons – Sediq, Rauf, and Dawalat – provide security services to a number of HNT contractors in the Gardez-Khost area.[103] According to one HNT contractor, Pacha Khan controls this region and it is not safe to operate there without paying his companies for security.[104] A former country manager of another HNT contractor reported to the military that Pacha Khan "controls who is able to access the bases to fulfill missions" and that his company was asked to pay a fee for trucks to pass through the area.[105]

Koka

Abdul Wali Khan, who goes by the name "Koka," is a warlord-cum-"police chief" in Musa Qala district, northern Helmand Province. His armed forces provide protection services for U.S. and NATO supply convoys over a wide swath of southern Afghanistan.

Only one HNT trucking company directly contracts with Koka for security, but others may do so indirectly through layers of subcontracting. Representatives of that company stated that Koka provides security to HNT trucks in and around forward operating base Dwyer.[106]

Koka has had a roller coaster relationship with coalition forces. In 2002, he was imprisoned by the U.S. for 14 months at Bagram jail "for suspected insurgent involvement."[107] After his release, by one press account, "he reappeared as a militia commander and lawman for the Afghan Government in Musa Qala, where by 2006 his tenure was marked by allegations of human rights abuses, killings and robberies."[108] According to the governor of Helmand, Koka took $20,000 a day in opium taxes and was involved in many mass murders.[109]

In 2006, the Taliban took over Helmand and the British forced President Karzai to remove Koka as a police official. According to the British commander at the time, "the UK does not want Koka here; all our good work could be undermined by the baggage he brings with him."[110]

In 2008, however, President Karzai strongly criticized the British for doing more harm than good by forcing the removal of Koka and other officials. "The mistake was that we removed a local arrangement without having a replacement. We removed the police force. That was not good."[111] Under pressure from President Karzai, the Afghan Ministry of Interior, and the Afghan National Army, the British relented, and Karzai reinstated Koka as police chief. Having no other choice, the British embraced him, even decorating the district with posters of Koka tending to a wounded civilian in front of a mountainous backdrop.[112]

Other Private Security Providers

Other private security providers for HNT convoys include Commander Rahim, Commander Masud, Commander Angar, Commander Habibullah Jan, Colonel Haji Toorjan, Gul Agha Sherzai, and General Gulalai.

2. The Highway Warlords Run a Protection Racket

Finding: The HNT contractors and their trucking subcontractors pay tens of millions of dollars annually to local warlords across Afghanistan in exchange for "protection" for HNT supply convoys to support U.S. troops. Although the warlords do provide guards and coordinate security, the contractors have little choice but to use them in what amounts to a vast protection racket. The consequences are clear: trucking companies that pay the highway warlords for security are provided protection; trucking companies that do not pay believe they are more likely to find themselves under attack. As a result, almost everyone pays. In interviews and documents, the HNT contractors frequently referred to such payments as "extortion," "bribes," "special security," and/or "protection payments."

Rashid Popal, the President of Watan Risk Management, praised Matiullah Khan lavishly. "Matiullah is a genius. Without him, Tarin Kowt [the capital of Uruzgan] would fall [to the Taliban]." According to Mr. Popal, Matiullah provides effective security and jobs for his province. He can do this because any contractor working there "must hire subcontractors and workers" from his province. Everyone, including Mr. Popal, must pay for Matiullah's security services to travel up the road from Kandahar to Tarin Kowt. There are no exceptions: "[n] o one leaves without paying... Matiullah will kill anyone on his highway, Taliban or not." A driver interviewed by the *New York Times* echoed that assessment: "It's suicide to come up this road without Matiullah's men."[113]

While a small handful of security companies apparently do operate convoy secruity missions on Highway 1 without paying Commander Ruhullah, they do so at their peril.

Along Highway 1, between Kabul and Kandahar, HNT contractors report that Commander Ruhullah runs a similar, but less effective, protection racket. To most trucking contractors, Commander Ruhullah "controls" Highway 1.

According to the former country manager of one HNT company that contracted with Watan, "you had to pay Ruhullah to either provide security or let [us] go through his territory." Commander Ruhullah held his company "hostage;" if he did not pay, he believed his trucks would be "shot up."[114]

While a small handful of security companies apparently do operate convoy security missions on this route without paying Commander Ruhullah, they do so at their peril. These companies report regular intimidation, "contact," and "surprises" that they attribute to Commander Ruhullah. While there is no comprehensive incident data to compare how each security company fares on Highway 1, there is widespread agreement among HNT contractors that those who do not use Commander Ruhullah face significantly greater risk.[115]

An executive from one private security company that travels Highway 1 without paying Commander Ruhullah said that U.S. supply convoys guarded by his company had come under attack by Commander Ruhullah's men on multiple occasions. "[He] was trying to scare us into not participating on his route, attacking our resolve to continue to service the route." He continued, "[Commander Ruhullah] operates with relative impunity from Ghazni to Kandahar, and even into Helmand Province... He is willing to ruthlessly exploit the lack of military control along the routes on which he operates."[116]

In an incident report from the summer of 2008, the security company reported hostile contact with 15-20 insurgents. According to the report:

> [The convoy security commander] came to the conclusion that this ambush... was well planned by Rohollah due to the following reason: When [the convoy security commander's] guards were moving with [the Ministry of Defense] convoy and Rohollah's guards, they were moving together till after Baghi Poul, when the convoy was at Howz-e-mdad, the rohollah's surfs [trucks] was in front of convoy and not with [the convoy security commander's] guards, they scattered themselves from [the convoy security commander's] guards. Close to Keskenadkhod, the surfs of Rohollah were in front of convoy, minutes before the ambush the guards of [the convoy security commander] could see that the guards of Rohollah were busy on their phones and now know that they were talking with the insurgents. Just before the ambush, 2 x Surfs (one of these Surfs as a black surf, the guards recognized this surf as the QRF for Rohollah's Ass commander) and 2 X Corolla's, **these vehicles came from the village and waited for Rohollah's surfs to pass before they started engaging with the weapons onto the guards of [the convoy security commander], that guards of Rohollah never returned fire onto the insurgents.**[117]

An HNT trucking contractor reported similar results. The company used Watan Risk Management with few major incidents in thousands of truck missions. On the handful of occasions that the company attempted to provide its own security on Highway 1, a senior executive reported that they "got shot up" and suspected Commander Ruhullah's fingerprints on the attack. For that company, the lesson was plain: "if we use Watan it works, if we use [our own] security it doesn't."[118]

Photo Credit: Subcommittee Staff

Documents and Correspondence Reflect a Vast Extortion Racketh

In a PowerPoint presentation dated May 9, 2009 (several days after performance of the HNT contract began), the country manager for one HNT prime contractor reported that his company was having trouble transporting goods to a U.S. forward operating base in Sharana, Paktika Province (key slide excerpted below) :[119]

When the military logisticians asked the prime contractors why they would not support missions to certain particularly insecure locations, the contractors vented about the high cost of "special security," and "protection payments." In a white paper submitted to the military in the Summer of 2009, one contractor complained about the high cost of security:[120]

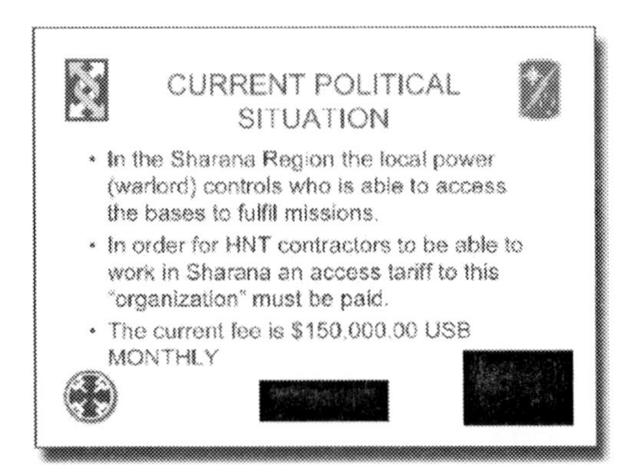

White Paper, [redacted] Dwyer Concerns/Leatherneck OP Area

<u>Security Costs</u>

Without being personally involved in the bidding on this contract I can confidently state that many of the costs of the increased volume focused in areas with difficult security situations was not factored in. The need to provide heavy weapons and robust security with ex pat leader leadership was not a requirement on the contract and now seems to be a requirement in some areas unless these missions are turned over to green security. I also believe that most involved in this contract knew that cash money is often the most effective security, but I do not think it was anticipated how high the market would drive these prices and that cash security and special security forces would so often be the only option.

RC South has been the location of nearly all of the attacks on IDIQ carriers, which needless to say presents significant challenges as it relates to controlling the quality of work and production from the LN drivers and security staff. The utilization of "Green Security" will eliminate the extortion in the south; however the attacks on convoys will increase due to this fact. Some carriers are paying as much as 15'000 dollars per truck for missions going to Dwyer and other south FOB, s. Green Security on these trips will be more cost effective, safer, and more efficient.

In response to the same Department of Defense request for information on security and costs on certain routes, another HNT project manager responded:

> The cost of security for these vehicles is very high and absorbs most of any profit we would make. Sub Contractors and drivers request more money to operate in this area, further adding to the problems for our companies... The cost of Private Security is exceptionally high, with companies attempting to raise their prices continually. **It is believed that a part of these charges are being paid as bribes to local Commanders, and therefore inevitably to the enemy**... As previously stated this is one of the most volatile regions of the country. There is a continuous threat of roadside IED, and ambush. **There**

will also be a threat, not only from enemy forces but from local commanders who have not been paid their tax.[121]

In an e-mail dated May 4, 2009 (within days of the beginning of the HNT contract), one HNT project manager wrote to his colleague: "the more dangerous the missions, entering areas where the Taliban controls, the more corruption we will have to deal with which for example requires an additional fee to get your trucks through without getting hit."[122]

In an e-mail dated June 9, 2009 between senior managers of the same contractor, the project manager wrote:

> I had a conversation with [the CEO of their trucking subcontractor] when I was devising the attached OP's plan and he became extremely offensive when I started asking him some very hard questions. Per a conversation he and I had last week we had 80 security vehicles so as you can see the plan is based on this number. When we got down to allocating vehicles per region per the plan he stated that we may not have 80 vehicles all the time. (what ever the F%$#! that means) **He then stated that the money that is allocated for the vehicles is sometimes utilized to pay the "Special Security" in the south and southwest so naturally I asked if we are using that money to pay them then why the F^%$#@ are we being charged 14,500 per truck going to the same areas, are we paying them twice?????????!!!! !! !!! !!**[123]

The contractor subsequently submitted a "request for equitable adjustment" to the Department of Defense to raise its contract price to account for the increased costs of "special security." The Department denied the request.

3. Protection Payments for Safe Passage Are a Significant Potential Source of Funding for the Taliban

Finding: Within the HNT contractor community, many believe that the highway warlords who nominally guard the trucks in turn make protection payments to insurgents to coordinate safe passage. This belief is evidenced in numerous documents, incident reports, and e-mails that refer to attempts at Taliban extortion along the road. The Subcommittee has not uncovered any direct evidence of such payments and Commander Ruhullah, the Popal brothers, and Ahmed Wali Karzai all adamantly deny that any convoy security commanders pay insurgents. According to experts and public reporting, however, the Taliban regularly extort rents from a variety of licit and illicit industries, and it is plausible that the Taliban would try to extort protection payments from the coalition supply chain that runs through territory in which they freely operate.

> *Every truck costs about $200 as a bribe I pay on the route – to police or Taliban. The Taliban don't care about small money: they ask for $10,000, $20,000 or $50,000 when they kidnap people.*
>
> – Haji Fata, CEO of Mirzada Transportation Company, as quoted in a November 13, 2009 Financial Times article, *High Costs to Get NATO Supplies Past Taliban*, by Matthew Green and Farhan Bokhari

Many within the HNT contractor community believe that a large portion of their protection payments to local warlords for convoy security subsequently go to the Taliban or other anti-government elements, the forces that actually control much of Afghanistan and many of the key routes used for transportation of U.S supplies. According to a former HNT project manager, it is widely known that the operational environment in Afghanistan requires payoffs to local warlords and the Taliban for safe passage of trucking convoys.[124]

A former employee of an HNT contractor that utilizes Watan Risk Management for security described a symbiotic relationship between Commander Ruhullah and the Taliban. According to this account, Commander Ruhullah only pays off Taliban forces if they are persistent enough to create a problem for Watan Risk Management guards on the road. Many firefights are really negotiations over the fee.[125] Another former HNT program manager who spent many years in the military said that he had "no doubt whatsoever" that Commander Ruhullah collaborated with insurgents.[126]

Asked whether Commander Ruhullah coordinated safe passage with insurgent groups, one security company executive stated:

> [W]e believe that Ruhullah serves his own needs at all times... We are of the opinion that, when it suits his need, he will engage with Taliban or similar elements. He will provide supplies and sell weapons to those elements but generally he is operating for his own benefits. So yes, he has links to [the Taliban] but he is not aligned with them. He doesn't consider himself a part of the Taliban.[127]

Documents Reflect Concern Regardging Taliban Extortion

Documents provided to the Subcommittee by the Department of Defense and contractors also reflect concerns regarding protection payments to hostile actors. For example, according to notes from a meeting of all HNT project managers and military logisticians, the participants specifically discussed protection payments "funding the insurgency":

> The PM [Project Manager] HNT from [an HNT contractor] asked LtCol Elwell if there was any progress on the Up Arming Authority [a request to be able to use greater armaments]. It was highlighted that this authority would enable IDIQ Carriers the flexibility to choose PSC to perform convoy security. **By gaining this authority IDIQ Carriers would stop funding the insurgency of what is estimated at 1.6 – 2 Million Dollars per week.**[128]

In an incident report filed by an HNT contractor in late 2007 (before the HNT contract started), the security manager wrote:

> Contacted through the carrier by the Taliban commander that we have to pay for safe passage if we want our truck to go through the area... [W] e were informed that this was a statement from the Taliban that if we did not want our assets engaged we had to pay a protection fee. [129]

In addition, as discussed in Finding 7, *infra*, many of the military logisticians that oversaw the contract were under the impression that the Taliban did receive protection payments, though this information was largely based on information provided to them by HNT contractor representatives.

Security Providers Deny Paying the Taliban

Commander Ruhullah and Watan Risk Management adamantly deny paying the Taliban. Rashid Popal stated that neither Watan nor convoy security companies could be "making deals" with the Taliban, and to suggest otherwise represented a lack of understanding of the Taliban's organizational structure. He argued that it would be "impossible to pay them off" because the Taliban is too decentralized and will not take money from "infidels."[130]

Commander Ruhullah pointed to his frequent firefights with the Taliban as evidence that he does not pay them. He claims to have lost 450 men in the last year alone and stated that his men had killed 20 Taliban in a major engagement earlier in the week. In the middle of his interview with Subcommittee staff, Commander Ruhullah received a call on his mobile phone and got up to speak in a hushed voice in the corner.[131] Later that day, his associate said that the sub-commander who had led the attack that killed the 20 Taliban had himself been slain in a retaliatory ambush. Commander Ruhullah had been informed of the slaying on the call during the interview, he said.[132]

Ahmed Wali Karzai also stated that private security companies were not paying the Taliban for safe passage. "It's impossible to pay everyone... The Taliban is not one any longer. There are different tribes and groups. One person does not control a 400 kilometer road. Maybe there is one leadership in Pakistan, but when you come down here, there are different tribes, different groups, different people." Mr. Karzai gave an example: "a guy in Helmand bought 30 dump trucks and paid one Taliban commander to get them through, but soon another [Taliban commander] heard of this and came and burnt all the trucks." [133]

Mr. Karzai argued that the increased danger on the road was partially a result of a *fatwa* issued by the Taliban that amounted to a "license to steal from Americans." As a result, there is no one group that could be bought off, but "hundreds and hundreds of groups trying to steal whatever they can along the road." Because unemployment is so high – and the fact that "an AK-47 is like a mobile phone, everyone has one" – the road has become virtual anarchy and the private security companies must fight their way through.

Discrepancies in Incident Reporting

According to the U.S. Army's 2006 "Counterinsurgency Manual," "[l] ogistic providers are often no longer the tail but the nose of a [counterinsurgency] force... Logistic units are perceived by insurgents as high-payoff targets and potential sources of supplies; thus lines of communications (LOCs) are a main battle area for insurgents."[134] Despite the insecurity of Afghanistan and the vulnerability of the supply lines there, many in the military believed that there were suspicious discrepancies in the incident rates for different HNT carriers and different security providers.[135]

Photo Credit: Militaryphotos.com

There is little hard data regarding the number and location of security incidents on the HNT contract in Afghanistan, and the data that is available is unreliable, but some evidence does support the discrepancies of concern to the military. For example, the manager of one HNT trucking company that used Watan Risk Management for much of its security said that his company had run over 10,000 truck missions from May 2009 to April 2010, but had only lost seven trucks and two drivers due to hostile action during that period.[136] Another contractor that also used Watan Risk Management had run roughly 15,000 missions from October 2009 to March 2010 but had only lost six trucks during the same period.[137] Meanwhile, other contractors were reporting a "high number of casualties."[138]

According to the former director of the Armed Contractor Oversight Directorate, his group had analyzed the incident reporting and determined that the discrepancies between companies reporting very low incident rates and companies reporting much higher incident rates was more than coincidence and should be further analyzed by the intelligence community.[139] If accurate, the low number of incidents reported by two of the carriers that were using Watan Risk Management for security would call into question the veracity of Commander Ruhullah's statement that he is engaged in daily gun battles with insurgents but failing to report them.

The Taliban Regularly Attempt to Extort from U.S. Contractors and Projects

According to U.S. officials, public reporting, and multiple experts, the Taliban regularly attempt to extort money from contractors for U.S. and coalition logistics and development work. Indeed, in December 2009, Secretary Clinton acknowledged before the Senate Foreign Relations Committee that "one of the major sources of funding for the Taliban is the protection money."[140]

Such protection payments are alleged to be widespread across a number of different industries in Afghanistan: reconstruction projects, telecommunications systems, poppy cultivation and smuggling, and transportation.[141]

A 2009 report on private security contractors in Afghanistan published by New York University alleged widespread protection payoffs to insurgents:

> Illicit taxation of PSPs [private security providers] escorting convoys and other scams on private transport and security are also an important source of funding for corrupt police and insurgents ... Although it is transportation

> and construction companies, both international and national, who are the main source of "protection" revenue, private security escorts also pay Taliban not to be attacked. According to an Afghan intelligence official, there are examples of PSPs paying as much as 60 percent of their gross profits for convoy security to the Taliban and other insurgent-cum-criminal groups for "protection."[142]

Several recent articles have described Taliban extortion of USAID-funded reconstruction projects. According to one author, the Afghan Threat Finance Cell, along with "military and embassy officials confirmed the insurgents also use extortion of U.S. development money for their funding, citing supply convoy shakedowns, construction protection rackets, Taliban 'taxes' on corrupt officials, pay-offs from NGOs and skims from poorly overseen government projects of the National Solidarity Program."[143] According to a quote attributed to a former security consultant in Afghanistan, "I have yet to find a security company that doesn't rely on payoffs to the Taliban."[144]

In another article, a journalist examined a small $200,000 dam and irrigation project: "In spite of the U.S. intervention in this Taliban-ridden region, the dam project has been counter-intuitively free of attack, leaving soldiers here suspicious. [Agri-business Development Team] commander Col. Brian Copes says: 'The Taliban might have taken 30 or 40 percent right off the top, and now [the contractor's] struggling to perform, because he's got less than 100 percent of budget because the Taliban took their cut right off the top.'"[145]

The Afghanistan country director for a major international NGO reported that "the Taliban and local warlords typically take between 10-20% of the value of any project as the price to provide protection. The United States and international community are unintentionally fueling a vast political economy of security corruption in Afghanistan."[146]

Allegations of protection payments are not limited to contractors. In October 2009, the *Times of London* reported that the U.S. Ambassador to Rome had launched a formal protest to the Italian government that their military had a regular practice of paying the Taliban tens of thousands dollars in bribes to maintain peace in Herat, an area under their supervision.[147] Reportedly, when the French took over the area from the Italians and did not pay these bribes, they came under immediate attack and ten soldiers died.[148] Prime Minister Berlusconi denied that his government had ever authorized such payments, although his administration was only three- months old when the transition from the Italians to the French took place.[149]

In the few public interviews with members of the Taliban, there is additional evidence that insurgents feed off of the massive influx of U.S. and coalition funds. A member of the Taliban publicly bragged in an interview that U.S. aid money funds their operations. When asked "what is the source of the Taliban's financing," he responded: "[f]rom U.S. dollars from the U.S. authorities!" He further explained, "[U.S. authorities] distribute dollars to the tribal chiefs, local administrators and other concerned people for welfare projects... Not every penny, but most goes into Taliban pockets to refuel their struggle."[150]

For his video series "Talking to the Taliban," journalist Graeme Smith conducted 42 video interviews with Taliban fighters. Mr. Smith concluded that "many kinds of negotiations with the Taliban have sprung up as the insurgents assert their presence in the outlying districts. Aid agencies and cell phone companies regularly negotiate safe passage of their workers across Taliban territory."[151]

Taliban Extortion of Other Industries

The Taliban's principal and most lucrative source of income in Afghanistan is its control of the opium trade. The Taliban have long profited off of the ten percent *ushr* tax levied on opium farmers, an additional tax on the traffickers, and a per-kilogram transit tariff charged to the truckers who transport the product. [152] In recent years, however, they have been "taking a page from the warlords' playbook," and regional and local Taliban commanders have been demanding "protection money from the drug traffickers who smuggle goods through their territory."[153] A 2007 analysis by the Jamestown Foundation described "arrangements whereby drug traffickers provide money, vehicles and subsistence to Taliban units in return for protection."[154] In addition, at even higher Taliban command levels, "senior leadership in Quetta are paid regular installments from narcotics kingpins as a general fee for operating in Taliban controlled areas."[155] Through these various forms of taxation and extortion, the Taliban have been estimated to earn nearly $300 million a year from the opium trade.[156]

While certainly the most lucrative, opium is not the only illicit business in Afghanistan and Pakistan from which the Taliban extorts payments to fund their operations. Throughout the Northwest Frontier Province (NWFP) and Federally Administered Tribal Areas (FATA) along Pakistan's border with Afghanistan, the Taliban have reportedly established a "symbiotic tie" with groups like the "timber mafia," for whom they serve as the "cavalry."[157]

In Afghanistan, the Taliban's ability to construct protection schemes extends beyond ungoverned, unprotected, or illicit industries. Since 2008, they have repeatedly extracted significant rents from the country's cell phone industry. According to several cell phone company executives quoted in a recent *Wall Street Journal* report, cell phone operators or their contractors "routinely disburse protection money to Taliban commanders."[158] These payments are in addition to money "openly passed to local tribal elders to protect a cell-tower site – cash that often ends up in Taliban pockets."[159]

In several provinces, including Kandahar, all of the national cell phone carriers (some of which are partly owned by major European companies) have made the joint decision to abide by a Taliban decree requiring them to shut off service from sun-down to sun-up. While the Taliban's ban was initially imposed to prevent potential informants from calling U.S. forces under the protection of darkness in order to provide tips on Taliban locations, it appears to have evolved into yet another form of extortion.

Amir Zai Sangin, the Afghan Minister of Communications, originally asked the companies to resist the Taliban's order. When the companies complied with the government's request and kept mobile service on during the evening, 40 telecommunications towers were destroyed at a cost of $400,000 each, and company employees were killed.[160] The government has since ceased demanding that the towers stay on at night. In a revealing admission, Mr. Sangin acknowledged that "there is no other way... We don't have the security to protect the towers."[161]

The Taliban's widespread extortion of people, businesses, contractors, NGOs, and criminal operations indicates that they are willing to finance their operations in whatever way possible, regardless of where those funds originate. With $2.16 billion being spent on the HNT contract, it is likely that the convoys would be yet another target for Taliban extortion.

4. Unaccountable Supply Chain Security Contractors Fuel Corruption

Finding: HNT contractors and their private security providers report widespread corruption by Afghan officials and frequent government extortion along the road. The largest private security provider for HNT trucks complained that it had to pay $1,000 to $10,000 in monthly bribes to nearly every Afghan governor, police chief, and local military unit whose territory the company passed. HNT contractors themselves reported similar corruption at a smaller scale, including significant numbers of ANP checkpoints. Military officials confirmed that they were aware of these problems.

Rashid Popal, the president of Watan Risk Management, raised his voice: "Why don't you ask me who I do pay?" After a number of questions regarding allegations of payments to the Taliban, Mr. Popal was eager to describe the real threat: "It is the government I am paying all along the way."[162] From Mr. Popal's perspective, the government, not the Taliban, "is the biggest threat to convoy security." Commander Ruhullah agreed. "Every government official is the enemy of these convoys," he declared.[163]

According to Commander Ruhullah and Watan Risk Management, bribes paid by drivers and security providers at Afghan National Army (ANA) and Afghan National Police (ANP) checkpoints represent only the tip of a pyramid of government corruption that feeds off of the U.S. supply chain. Rashid Popal quickly volunteered a list of government offices that his company must bribe in order to successfully escort HNT convoys along Highway 1, including governors, provincial police chiefs, district police chiefs, and local commanders for the National Directorate of Security, in addition to the local ANA and ANP units. Many of the bribes are paid monthly and range from $1,000 to $ 10,000.[164]

"Every government official is the enemy of these convoys."

– Commander Ruhullah

If the warlords and security companies are so powerful, why pay? According to the Popals, security companies view these bribes as "nuisance payments" because local government officials can make operations difficult for them. The government's ability to "deregister" private security contractors is of particular concern, which gives officials who control the licensing process significant power. Officials not able to leverage their authority on the licensing process simply impose "new laws and regulations on a daily basis." This is standard procedure according to Commander Ruhullah, who said that police chiefs and governors did their best to structure laws in a way that enabled them to extort the convoys that passed through their areas of jurisdiction.[165] Commander Ruhullah gave an example: a new requirement in one area that all convoys wait until 10:00 p.m. to depart, forcing the convoys to travel during the more dangerous nighttime and giving local officials a full day to extort bribes. Another common practice of police harassment, he said, is to stop convoys and check every single guard's weapon for proper registration papers.[166]

Other government interventions cited by Watan Risk Management were more sinister. Rashid Popal claimed that a member of the Afghan Parliament had attempted to enlist Haji Musah, a "legendary fighter" and member of Hizb-I Islami Gulbuddin, an Islamist political and military group, in an attempt to muscle Commander Ruhullah and Watan Risk Management out of the convoy security business in one province.[167]

Rashid Popal stated that he had once asked a provincial governor why he forced Watan Risk Management to pay bribes even though the company had helped to improve the security of his province. According to Mr. Popal, the governor explained quite simply that he was forced to extort money from the private security companies in order to pay back what he had paid for his position. The same rules apply to police chiefs and other government officials who pay a set price to the provincial government in order to obtain their positions, said Mr. Popal.[168]

Other security and trucking contractors portrayed a more cooperative, albeit still corrupt, relationship between security companies and the ANA/ANP. One HNT contractor stated that Commander Ruhullah pays local ANA commanders as much as $300,000 per month to supplement Watan's security forces.[169] A security company executive concurred, stating that Commander Ruhullah "operates with corrupt members of ANP and ANA to achieve his desired outcomes," which often includes attacking or directly disrupting the operations of other security companies.[170] Commander Ruhullah flatly denied employing active ANA/ANP officers to work on his convoys, saying that he was only forced to pay bribes.[171]

Many of the HNT contractors also acknowledged that trucking convoys were forced to pay bribes to all manner of government officials at various stages along the road. The CEO of one HNT contractor said that his drivers are frequent targets of ANA and ANP extortion because they carry emergency cash reserves for breakdowns. He said that he issued specific orders to truck drivers not to pay bribes to the ANA and ANP and that his trucks had been impounded as a result, requiring him to go out personally by helicopter to free his drivers. The ANA and ANP know that the drivers carry between $400 and $1,000, he said, but in a cash-based society the drivers have no other option to pay for food, fuel, tires, and cranes in case of an accident. In Afghanistan, "every driver ... must be self-sufficient on the road." As a result, many of his drivers pay the bribes out of fear.[172]

Another HNT contractor's country manager said that he had heard of "bribery and extortion by government officials," such as "checkpoints by ANP that request money" from drivers, but said that his drivers rarely speak about the payoffs and each believes that his "life is in danger if he reveals information."[173]

Military officials with oversight of the HNT contract were also aware of widespread allegations of official Afghan government corruption. Lieutenant Colonel Lewis, the HNT manager for the 143rd Expeditionary Sustainment Command, stated that he had heard significant reports regarding alleged bribes to the ANA outside of Kandahar Airfield. He took an armored vehicle and went to observe for himself, but he could tell that the ANA acted differently with him around.[174]

Lieutenant Colonel Elwell, the commander of the 484th Movement Control Battalion that directly managed the HNT contract, also reported that he was aware of unauthorized police checkpoints outside of Kandahar Airfield. Lieutenant Colonel Elwell stated that he had wanted to investigate official corruption further but it was difficult because the checkpoints moved frequently.[175]

5. Unaccountable Supply Chain Security Contractors Undermine U.S. Counterinsurgency Strategy

> **Finding:** While outsourcing principal responsibility for the supply chain in Afghanistan to local truckers and unknown security commanders has allowed the Department of Defense to devote a greater percentage of its force structure to priority operations, these logistics arrangements have significant unintended consequences for the overall counterinsurgency strategy. By fueling unaccountable warlords and funding parallel power structures, the United States undercuts efforts to establish popular confidence in a credible and sustainable Afghan government.

In both conventional and irregular war, the normal rule of law – and attendant mechanisms for oversight and punishment – has deteriorated. As a result, the use of deadly force must be entrusted only to those whose training, character and accountability are most worthy of the nation's trust: the military. The military profession carefully cultivates an ethic of "selfless service," and develops the virtues that can best withstand combat pressures and thus achieve the nation's objectives in an honorable way. By contrast, most corporate ethical standards and available regulatory schemes are ill-suited for this environment. We therefore conclude that contractors should not be deployed as security guards, sentries, or even prison guards within combat areas. [Armed private security guards] should be restricted to appropriate support functions and those geographic areas where the rule of law prevails. In irregular warfare environments, where civilian cooperation is crucial, this restriction is both ethically and strategically necessary.

– Letter from Vice Admiral Jeff Fowler, Superintendent, U.S. Naval Academy
to General James T. Conway, Commandant of the Marine Corps summarizing the
2009 McCain Conference on Ethics & Military Leadership

During the Soviet Union's ten-year war in Afghanistan, "[h] ardly a day would pass without a Mujahideen attack on enemy columns along the main highway connecting [Kandahar] with Ghazni." Much of the combat for the entire conflict gravitated around control and protection of the thinly stretched Soviet supply chain. More than three-fourths of Soviet combat forces were regularly involved in convoy security missions, which prevented them from ever sustaining a larger occupation force and controlling key cities such as Kandahar.[176]

In Afghanistan, the U.S. Department of Defense has created a new model of supply chain that relies entirely on private local contractors to carry and defend the food, water, shelter, fuel, and arms that our troops need to perform their mission. The logistics benefits of such a supply chain model are clear – U.S. troops are not put directly in harms way for logistics missions and can instead focus on higher priority objectives – but the costs to overall U.S. counterinsurgency strategy have not been adequately analyzed or assessed. As one former senior Department of Defense official in Kabul put it: "[t]his is symptomatic of what we are doing [in Afghanistan]. Our heart is in the right place, but the business model is to outsource important services and not look at the collateral consequences."[177]

"They Tend to Squeeze the Trigger First and Ask Questions Later"

In August 2009, General Stanley McChrystal released his "Commander's Initial Assessment" of NATO forces in Afghanistan where he declared that, "success demands a comprehensive counterinsurgency campaign" to gain "the support of the Afghan people." The assessment then specifically outlined how unrestrained, arbitrary force negatively impacts counterinsurgency efforts. Civilian casualties and collateral damage resulting "from an over-reliance on firepower and force protection have severely damaged ISAF's legitimacy in the eyes of the Afghan people." The assessment concluded that the Afghans perceived that ISAF was "complicit" in "widespread corruption and abuse of power."[178]

Screenshot of Watan Risk Management guards engaged in a firefight off Highway 1

While the Department of Defense may not know who operates and protects its supply chain, the Afghan people do. When a supply convoy of 300 trucks and 500 heavily armed guards rolls down Highway 1 engaging in firefights with competitors, criminals, and insurgents, the local population understands that it is an American convoy.[179] In other words, in the eyes of the Afghan population, the United States of America is responsible for the actions of Commander Ruhullah, Matiullah, Colonel Razziq, Koka, and others.

A recent article entitled, "Reckless Private Security Companies Anger Afghans," painted a portrait of U.S. military operators' frustration with the unaccountable private security companies protecting NATO supplies that travel through their battlespace:

> Private Afghan security guards protecting NATO supply convoys in southern Kandahar province regularly fire wildly into villages they pass, hindering coalition efforts to build local support ahead of this summer's planned offensive in the area, U.S. and Afghan officials say.
>
> The guards shoot into villages to intimidate any potential militants, the officials say, but also cause the kind of civilian casualties that the top U.S. commander in Afghanistan has tried repeatedly to stop.
>
> "Especially as they go through the populated areas, they tend to squeeze the trigger first and ask questions later," said Capt. Matt Quiggle, a member of the U.S. Army's 5th Stryker brigade tasked with patrolling Highway One, which connects Afghanistan's major cities.

The troops say they have complained to senior coalition officials and have even detained some guards to lecture them about their conduct, but the problem has continued.

Many suspect there has been little response because the security companies are owned by or connected to some of the province's most powerful figures...

Public anger is directed at the Afghan government and coalition forces, making it more difficult for the U.S. and others to convince locals that they should look to them for protection rather than the Taliban, said Lt. Col. Dave Abrahams, deputy commander of a Stryker battalion that patrols the stretch of Highway One...

"The irresponsible actions of these companies" are jeopardizing NATO's attempts to gain the support of local villagers, Abrahams wrote in an e-mail to his superiors late last year.

"They are armed, wearing uniforms, escorting U.S. convoys, and indiscriminately shooting into villages," said Abrahams, deputy commander of the 2nd Battalion, 1st Infantry Regiment, 5th Stryker Brigade, 2nd Infantry Division...

Abrahams, the deputy battalion commander, tried to address the problem in November by stopping two convoys as they passed his base.

"We basically detained their entire security force, and I sat down to talk to their leaders to tell them not to shoot without reason and basically threatened" to take away their certification to work for NATO, said Abrahams. "But we haven't been able to make good on it, which is part of our frustration."

Many of the gunmen have little or no training and many are also high on either heroin or hashish, Afghan and U.S. officials said...

Abrahams said he has tried to tell locals that he understands their plight, but he is consistently undermined by the wild shooting.

"Actions speak louder than words, and the locals see these drugged-out thugs with guns and trucks with 'The United States' painted on the side," said Abrahams.[180]

"Actions speak louder than words, and the locals see these drugged-out thugs with guns and trucks with 'The United States' painted on the side."

– U.S. Lieutenant Colonel Dave Abrahams

The NATO commander of Regional Command-South, British Major General Nick Carter, agreed with the Highway 1 Stryker Battalion assessment, describing private security contractors as operating in a "culture of impunity."[181]

Warlords Are a "Parallel Structure to the Government"

> *Units Employing [host nation] contractors and employees must watch for signs of exploitive or corrupt business practices that may alienate segments of the local populace and inadvertently undermine [counterinsurgency] objectives.*
>
> – General David Petraeus and General James Amos, Counterinsurgency, Department of the Army (December 2006)

According to Qayum Karzai, President Karzai's brother and an Afghan-American businessman, "the majority of money that should have gone to the Afghan people has gone to warlords and they are more powerful now than they have ever been." In an interview with Subcommittee staff, Mr. Karzai lamented that warlords are "much more difficult to deal with now than they were nine years ago," and described them as the "single element that has sidelined the population." The population lost trust in "traditional Afghan political culture when warlords took over." "[The Afghan people] saw the fight between warlords and Taliban, and they disliked both of them."[182]

Qayum Karzai, Ahmed Wali Karzai, Rashid and Ahmed Rateb Popal, and Commander Ruhullah all agreed that, in a perfect world, the ANA and ANP should provide security along the roads, but that such security would be a long time off. In the meantime, Watan Risk Management and Commander Ruhullah are engaged in active – and sometimes hostile – competition with the government. Commander Ruhullah described the Afghan government as "the enemy of convoy security."[183]

> ***"The Afghan people saw the fight between warlords and Taliban, and they dislikedboth."***
>
> – Qayum Karzai

In Uruzgan Province, for example, providing a variety of security services to the U.S. and NATO forces has significantly increased the power of Matiullah Khan vis-à-vis the official Afghan government structures there. According to the *New York Times*, "[m]any Afghans say the Americans and their NATO partners are making a grave mistake by tolerating or encouraging warlords like Mr. Matiullah. These Afghans fear the Americans will leave behind an Afghan government too weak to do its work, and strongmen without any popular support."[184]

The Afghan government also seems to share concerns about the growing power of warlords at the expense of their own authority and legitimacy. The former Minister of the Interior, Hanif Atmar, stated, "[p] arallel structures of government create problems for the rule of law." As one tribal elder in Uruzgan put it, "Matiullah is not part of the government, he is stronger than the government, and he can do anything he wants."[185]

In short, while one of the primary U.S. strategic goals in Afghanistan is to bolster the Afghan central government, U.S. reliance on warlords for supply chain security has the effect of dramatically undermining that objective.

6. The Department of Defense Lacks Effective Oversight of Its Supply Chain and Private Security Contractors in Afghanistan

Finding: The Department of Defense has little to no visibility into what happens to the trucks carrying U.S. supplies between the time the trucks leave the gate to the time they arrive at their destination. Despite serious concerns regarding operations, no military managers have ever observed truck operations on the road or met with key security providers. The Department of Defense's regulations, promulgated in response to direction by Congress, require oversight of all private security companies working as contractors or subcontractors for the U.S government. These requirements include ensuring that all private security company personnel comply with U.S. government and local country firearm laws, that all private security company equipment be tracked, and that all incidents of death, injury, or property damage be fully investigated. The Department of Defense is grossly out of compliance with applicable regulations and has no visibility into the operations of the private security companies that are subcontractors on the HNT contract.

The HNT contract is worth $2.16 billion and covers 70 percent of the supply chain for the U.S. effort in Afghanistan. The contract is critical to the basic survival of U.S. troops stationed throughout the country in remote and dangerous areas. By any measure, a contract of this significance would seem to demand exacting oversight by the Department of Defense. Both military and HNT contractor personnel reported that such oversight was virtually nonexistent.

The Military Contract Overseers Had "Zero Visiblity"

The 484th Joint Movement Control Battalion was responsible for managing and overseeing HNT missions from May 2009 (when the contract started) to February 2010. According to Lieutenant Colonel David Elwell, the commander of the 484th, no one in the battalion ever personally witnessed trucking operations 'outside the wire' – outside of the major airfields and forward operating bases where supplies are uploaded and downloaded. The 484th did not have the "force structure, the equipment, or the security" to put eyes on the road. "It would have been a combat mi ssi on."[186]

Several other members of the 484th confirmed that they were unable to effectively oversee the operations of the HNT contract. According to Major Valen Koger, the officer responsible for technical oversight of the contract, his battalion had "zero visibility" into the subcontractors operating under the contract. During his almost one-year tour in Afghanistan, he rarely left Bagram Airfield, and he stated that he could not verify any reports of what was actually happening on the road. Major Koger expressed concern that, as the person responsible for oversight on behalf of the contracting office, he could not actually oversee many aspects of the HNT contract. [187]

The Battle Captain, whose job it was to monitor incidents and track incident reporting, stated that it was difficult to verify incidents that occurred on the roads. Although he heard rumors that contractors had to bribe "warlords" to get through certain areas, he did not know who these men were and did not have any visibility into their identities beyond what was reported to him by the prime contractors.[188]

The contracting office at RCC-Bagram was equally unaware of the operations of the subcontractors used by the HNT prime contractors. The contracting office was responsible for vetting the contractors and awarding the HNT contracts.[189] Once operations began, the contracting officers were responsible for ensuring that all provisions of the HNT contract were being followed by the contractors.[190] Two former contracting officers stated that they communicated regularly with the prime contractors, but did not have a direct way to check on their operations. Both of these contracting officers relied exclusively on reports from the 484th and the HNT prime contractors for information regarding whether the contractors were in compliance with the contract. Neither ever went out on the road themselves to observe these operations.[191]

For information about the HNT operations, the 484th largely relied on reports from the HNT prime contractors themselves. Very few of the prime contractor representatives (the Western expats who interface with the military) have ever seen a trucking mission first-hand, however. Instead, most of the HNT representatives rely on their Afghan trucking subcontractors to tell them what happens on the road. This information is often less than reliable. Frequently, the HNT prime contractors' subcontractors further subcontract out the missions without the knowledge of the primes. Although they claim to have their own trucks, many of the principal subcontractors are nothing more than brokerages for tribal trucking firms or owner-operators.[192]

Thus, the military officials responsible for oversight and management of the HNT contract have no reliable way of knowing what is actually happening on the road.

Required Oversight of Private Security Contractors

In 2008, following widespread media reports of severe misconduct by private security contractors working for the U.S. military in Iraq and Afghanistan, Congress included a section in the National Defense Authorization Act for Fiscal Year 2008 (FY08 NDAA)[193] that required the Department of Defense and the Department of State to promulgate regulations to improve oversight and accountability of private security contractors (PSCs). Congress mandated that the regulations include, *inter alia*, processes for:

1. Registering, tracking, and keeping records of personnel working for PSCs or otherwise providing private security services;
2. Authorizing and accounting for weapons used by such personnel;
3. Registering military vehicles used by PSCs;
4. Mandatory reporting by PSCs of all incidents in which PSC personnel discharge a weapon, PSC personnel are killed or injured, and others are killed or injured, or property is destroyed, as a result of actions by PSC personnel;
5. Independent review and investigation, where practicable, of any reported incidents as well as any allegations of misconduct by a PSC; and
6. Training and qualifying PSC personnel.

Congress also mandated that all contracts for private security contractors include a clause requiring the companies to comply with Department of Defense regulations as well as applicable local and U.S. law. While these regulations are limited to private security contractors operating in areas of combat as designated by the Secretary of Defense, Congress included language to ensure Iraq and Afghanistan would be included.

Department of Defense Instruction 3020.50, *Private Security Contractors Operating in Contingency Operations*, which was signed on July 22, 2009, lays out the policy and regulations pursuant to the requirements of the FY08 NDAA. The Instruction policies apply to "DoD [Department of Defense] PSCs and PSC personnel performing private security functions during contingency operations outside the United States" and "U.S.G.-funded PSCs and PSC personnel performing private security functions in an area of combat operations." The Instruction defines the term "contractor" as "the contractor, subcontractor, grantee, or other party carrying out the covered contract." In other words, private security contractors working under the HNT contract are covered by this Instruction.

In addition to the main provisions, noted above, that are required by the FY08 NDAA, the Instruction includes extensive provisions related to the arming of private security contractor personnel. Under these regulations, the companies must verify that their personnel meet the legal, training, and qualification requirements to carry a weapon under the contract and local law. Requests to arm private security contractor personnel are to be reviewed on a case-by-case basis by a Staff Judge Advocate. All such requests must include, *inter alia*, a communication plan for how information about threats will be shared between private security contractors personnel and the U.S. military, and how the military will provide assistance to private security contractors who become involved in hostile situations. Private security contractors must acknowledge in writing that, among other things, they can only carry U.S. government-issued and/or -approved weapons and ammunition.

While the Department's Instruction does not appear to assign the responsibility of monitoring and enforcing compliance to any particular entity, the FY08 NDAA gives contracting officers, in addition to combatant commanders, the power to direct contractors to remove noncompliant personnel, and to terminate contracts for repeated violations.

Finally, section (i) of the Joint Contracting Command - Iraq/Afghanistan clause 952.225-001 instructs that "all arming requests and authorizations for contractor or subcontractor employees under this contract shall be *limited to* U.S. Government-approved weapons and ammunition." [194] The clause defines "U.S. Government-approved weapons and ammunition" as "M9, M4, M16, or equivalent (e.g. .45 CAL, AK-47)." [195] An August 2009 JCC-I/A Policy Directive instructed that this clause "shall be included in all contracts with performance in Iraq or Afghanistan that require arming of contractors."[196]

No Oversight of HNT Private Security Contractors

Despite Congress's clear intention that the Department of Defense monitor, account for, and, when necessary, discipline private security contractors, the security providers working on the HNT contract are not subjected to any meaningful oversight by the U.S. military. The Department has even less visibility into security operations on the road than it does on the trucking missions themselves. For security reasons, private security contractors for HNT missions are not allowed 'inside the wire' with the trucks they are guarding. In most cases, the security providers and the trucks meet up many miles outside the base, or even in separate provinces. As such, none of the military's HNT managers or overseers ever witness security operations in action. As with the trucking operations themselves, HNT managers rely on the prime contractor representatives to tell them who provides security for Department of Defense's supplies and how that security is provided. Most of the prime contractors dutifully provide what they know, but that information is rarely comprehensive or fully accurate.

Lieutenant Colonel Elwell confirmed that the 484th had "very little visibility" into the security operations of the HNT contractors. He stated that the 484th regularly emphasized the security requirements to the carriers, but there was very little that the 484th could do to verify that proper licensing and vetting of guards was actually taking place since security elements could not come 'inside the wire.' Once the trucks left the bases and met up with security, the 484th had no direct way to verify that security was actually continuing with the trucks, or if that security was licensed.[197]

The Armed Contractor Oversight Directorate

Since 2008, the Armed Contractor Oversight Directorate (ACOD) has been responsible for regulating and overseeing private contractors employed under U.S. contracts in Afghanistan, including those working as subcontractors. Despite being charged with tracking private security contractors, the former Director of ACOD, who left Afghanistan in December 2009, reported that ACOD was unable to oversee the private security contractors working on the HNT contract. He found that, in most cases, the prime contractors subcontracted out security, and those security subcontractors further subcontracted out security operations. He knew, for example, that Watan Risk Management provides security to several HNT contractors, but he had no knowledge of how Watan operates. He said that "anyone who is receiving DoD dollars should be tracked," but ACOD had not been able to do so.[198]

The current Director of ACOD, Colonel Son Le, also agreed that ACOD does not have visibility into the operations of HNT security providers. He stated that he relied on the prime contractors to ensure proper security operations were being carried out.[199]

Few HNT Prime Contractors Know What Happens on the Road

Because the military contract officials do not have direct oversight into the security operations on HNT missions, they rely on reports by the prime contractors. However, in many cases the prime contractors themselves have little knowledge of the actual security arrangements for their convoys. For security reasons, most of the prime contractor representatives are unable or unwilling to travel out on the roads. One HNT program manager stated that he has no direct knowledge of how security operations for his company's missions are conducted because his company's personnel do not travel with convoys or interact directly with the security elements.[200] A former country manager for another HNT contractor stated that he never went out on the roads due to the danger of doing so and that he did not interact with the company that provided security for his company's convoys.[201]

Several contractors leave it entirely up to their trucking subcontractors to arrange for convoy security.[202] A country manager for one contractor confirmed that his trucking subcontractor generally coordinates all security operations for convoys.[203]

As an illustration of prime contractors' lack of knowledge about their own operations, in response to questions by the 484th and the contracting office regarding security operations on its convoys, one contractor sent two e-mails in the same month that identified two different sets of security providers used by the company's subcontractors. In a December 2, 2009 e-mail, a program manager for the contractor identified its security providers as "Rohulla Escort," "Afghanistan Naveen," "Rahim Escort," and "Commander Mansoor Escort."[204] In a December 23, 2009 e-mail, another program manager for the same company identified the security providers as "Com Malik," "Rohullah," "Habibullah," "Naween Security Company," and "Zadran Security Company."[205]

Higher Command

The 143rd Expeditionary Sustainment Command sat above the 484th on the contract management chain of command. The 143rd was consulted on many of the HNT challenges and assigned an HNT program manager, Lieutenant Colonel Todd Lewis, to help perform oversight on the contract. Although he tried to figure out what was happening 'outside the wire,' Lieutenant Colonel Lewis was never able to successfully do so. He could not get authorization to go to key highways to witness trucking operations first hand because such a trip would require too much security. He called his inability to get information on HNT trucking and security operations the single biggest frustration from his service in Afghanistan.[206]

The 484th also worked with the Principal Assistant Responsible for Contracting-Afghanistan (PARC-A).[207] Colonel Daniel Cottrell, the PARC-A, stated that it was the responsibility of the prime contractors to ensure that security was properly provided.[208]

Subcommittee staff traveling with a congressional delegation in January 2010 met with several other senior military officials, including Major General John MacDonald and his team of senior military logistics officers, regarding the HNT contract. Major General MacDonald admitted that the Department of Defense did not have visibility into the operations of the trucking companies or their security providers and that this was an issue of concern.[209]

In summary, neither the critical importance of the HNT contract, the significant value of the contract (especially in relation to the economy of Afghanistan), nor the legal and regulatory requirements have been sufficient to prompt the Department of Defense to devote the resources necessary to properly oversee the contractors, subcontractors, and private security providers who operate the supply chain.

7. HNT Contractors Warned the Department of Defense about Protection Payments for Safe Passage to No Avail

Finding: In meetings, interviews, e-mails, white papers, and PowerPoint presentations, many HNT prime contractors self-reported to military officials and criminal investigators that they were being forced to make "protection payments" for "safe passage" on the road. While military officials acknowledged receiving the warnings, these concerns were never appropriately addressed.

Under normal circumstances, contractors do not volunteer to the government that they might be breaking the law; in this case, HNT contractors repeatedly did just that. Their reports fell on deaf ears.

Representatives for the HNT contractors regularly informed military officials that they were concerned that money was going to "insurgents," "warlords," other local actors, and corrupt government officials.[210] These warnings were met with apparent inaction. Although many military officials later expressed concerns to the Subcommittee staff about what they had heard, little action was ever taken to investigate or address the issue.[211] From the logisticians' perspective, their jobs were to make sure the goods got to where they needed to go. Any other concerns were beyond the scope of their duty.

Though Lieutenant Colonel Elwell and the 484th were in charge of direct management and oversight of the HNT contract, responsibility for oversight did not end there. Senior military commanders and other Department of Defense components were aware of the same allegations of protection payments for safe passage but failed to take action.

Early Warnings about Highway Extortion

Before the HNT contract began in early 2009, one current HNT contractor had already warned the military of being approached by "Taliban personnel" about safe passage payments. The contractor sent a memorandum to the military manager to record a Taliban request for "payment for the safe passage of convoys through there [sic] area... We have talked to other carriers that are making missions through those areas and they are paying the Taliban for safe passage."[212]

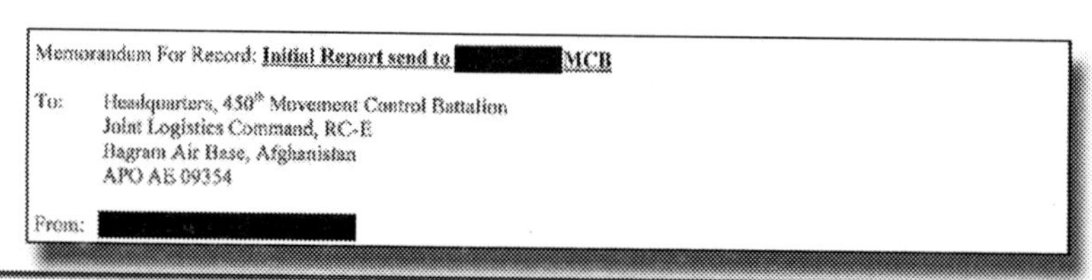

Memorandum For Record: **Initial Report send to [redacted] MCB**

To: Headquarters, 450th Movement Control Battalion
Joint Logistics Command, RC-E
Bagram Air Base, Afghanistan
APO AE 09354

From: [redacted]

[redacted] was approached by Taliban personnel to talk about payment for the safe passage of convoys through there area. [redacted]'s policy is that we will not pay extortion money to fund their weapons or training to kill American Service men and women conducting operations in Afghanistan. If we make payment that money will be funneled back into their fight against the Coalition and our principles on that matter are straight forward. We have talked to other carriers that are making missions through those areas and they are paying the Taliban for safe passage. The current price to the Taliban is $500 per truck from Kandahar to Herat. $50 from Kabul to Ghazni, $100 from Ghazni to Orguni, and $200-$300 from Orguni to Waza Kwah. All negotiations are conducted outside of Afghanistan and for the southern and western areas the Taliban POC is located in Quetta Pakistan.

Within days of the start of the HNT contract in May 2009, contractors informed military officials that they were being asked to make protection payments for safe passage through critical areas in the south and east. On May

9, 2009, the country manager for one HNT contractor submitted a PowerPoint presentation detailing the challenges his company faced in transporting goods to Forward Operating Base Sharana in Paktika Province. He reported that a local warlord controlled access to the bases, contractors were being asked to pay a "tariff" to gain access, and the fee was $150,000 per month (key slide is excerpted in Finding 2).[213]

The presentation was sent to several military officials, including Major Koger at the 484th. The country manager said that he created and sent the presentation because he did not feel comfortable funding a warlord's private militia without the military's permission. He recalled telling Major Koger that either the military had to fix the situation with the warlord or otherwise provide written permission for the contractor to make the payments. The country manager said that Major Koger had been sympathetic to his concerns, but when Major Koger took it up his chain of command, he was surprised and disappointed that the "higher ups just didn't want to hear it."[214]

Major Koger did not recall the PowerPoint presentation but agreed that it had probably been sent to him. He explained that the general view held by many at the 484th was that such contractor complaints were simply part of a "pattern of excuses" for poor performance on the HNT contract.[215]

The contracting officer for the HNT contract at the inception of performance recalled multiple contractors telling her that they were making protection "payments to the wrong side." "There were a lot of requests for bribes along the road, like tolls, to bandits, Taliban, whomever," she stated. The contracting officer said that she believed the contractors when they told her that the protection payments were taking place because the contractors did not have any other reason to self-report potentially illegal activity. "[E]verybody was well aware" of the protection payment issue.[216]

Regular Complaints about Protection Payments Met a Brick Wall

Several of the HNT contractors recalled that they reported their concerns of being extorted and making bribes out on the roads at several regular monthly meetings with the 484th and contracting officers.[217] One program manager reported these concerns at a July 9, 2009 meeting where representatives from the military and all of the HNT contractors were present.[218] After that meeting, the program manager e-mailed meeting minutes to all of the other HNT contractors as well as members of the 484th , including Lieutenant Colonel Elwell and Major Koger.[219] The contractors were seeking to gain up-arming authority for their private security contractors to carry heavier weapons such as RPGs and heavy machine guns to counter insurgent attacks, and the program manager reported that gaining this up-arming authority was the only way for the companies to stop making payments to insurgents.[220] The meeting notes state:

Host Nation Trucking Monthly JMCB Meeting

Tuesday 7th July 2009

484th Joint Movement Control Battalion Conference Room, Bagram Air Field

Meeting Commenced at: 1002hrs

Up arming authority

11. The PM HNT from ▇▇ asked LtCol Elwell if there was any progress on the Up Arming Authority. It was highlighted that this authority would enable IDIQ Carriers the flexibility to choose PSC to perform convoy security. By gaining this authority IDIQ Carriers would stop funding the insurgency of what is estimated at 1.6 – 2 Million Dollars per week. Lieutenant Colonel Elwell had no information regarding the progress and his response to the estimated cost IDIQ Carriers were funding the insurgency was that all he cared about was that the cargo was delivered in accordance with the contract.

Major Koger did not recall seeing the meeting minutes, but he described their account of the July 9, 2009 meeting as "accurate." He stated that he had spoken to several of the contractors about their concerns regarding demands for protection payments but that he believed that the problem had probably been occurring for years and would have already been resolved if a feasible solution existed. Major Koger characterized his overall level of concern regarding the reports of protection payments as "extremely concerned," but his advice to contractors on how to deal with the situation was unhelpful: he told them that there was nothing in the contract that authorized paying "extortion money."[221]

Lieutenant Colonel Elwell said that the meeting minutes mischaracterized his comments, but he acknowledged that the HNT contractor representatives had complained at that meeting and on numerous other occasions about protection payments. He "clearly" recalled that the contractors had complained about the high cost of security at that meeting, but they never said that the protection payments were going to insurgents. His response to those costs was that the contractors had known the risks when they took on the contract and needed to perform without making excuses.[222]

Like Major Koger, Lieutenant Colonel Elwell emphasized that he very clearly told the contractors that all private security providers needed to be licensed and vetted in accordance with the contract. He also seemingly discouraged further communications to him about safe passage payments by telling the contractors that if they were not in compliance with the security provisions of the contract, he would have to convey that information to the contracting office, whose only power in these circumstances would be to punish noncompliance with the contract.[223]

> ***"Investigating protection payments was way, way, way, way above my level. My job was to get barrels of insulating foam for tents out to to Dwyer so Marines didn't suffocate fromheat exhaustion."***
>
> – Lieutenant Colonel Elwell

Lieutenant Colonel Elwell took comfort that, despite the "constant whining" from carriers about security costs, "he never had any official communication from the carriers saying they were paying protection money to insurgents." To him, unless an issue was raised in "official correspondence," it was just rumor and hearsay.[224]

Although Lieutenant Colonel Elwell had never 'left the wire' and traveled on the roads, he held strong views about how Afghanistan actually functioned. He believed that some contractors mistook support for local tribes as support for the insurgency. "The statement that Taliban were helping to secure convoys would not necessarily signal to me that insurgents were doing this. A lot of former Taliban were working for legitimate businesses and providing legitimate security services."[225]

Even if they had wanted to, the contract managers of the 484th did not have the means to investigate allegations of protection payments for safe passage. As Lieutenant Colonel Elwell put it: "That was way, way, way, way above my level. My job was to get barrels of insulating foam for tents out to Dwyer so Marines didn't suffocate from heat exhaustion."[226]

The contractor representatives who self-reported to the 484th and the military contracting officers that their companies were making protection payments for safe passage were shocked by the lack of response from the military. One former program manager said that he expected that his complaints would "set off alarm bells at DoD," but instead the response was "I don't care." In his view, none of the prime contractors knew where their security payments were going. He believed that the warlords provided some legitimate security services, but "there was also a certain element of extortion.

If you don't pay a certain person to secure a route for you [then you would be attacked]." After having spent over 20 years in the military including service in Afghanistan, the program manager said that he had "no doubt whatsoever" that warlords like Commander Ruhullah coordinated such attacks with insurgents.[227]

A former country manager stated that he had raised the issue of protection payments for safe passage through "every official channel" he could, except for the U.S. Embassy in Kabul. He said that he raised the issue with operators on the ground and the intelligence community. He was met with a lot of sympathy but never any action.[228] As someone who had spent many years in the U.S. Special Forces, the prospect of funding warlords and potentially insurgents was "repugnant" to him. As a result, he left Afghanistan.

No-Go Areas

The contractors' concerns regarding protection payments for safe passage received more attention when the contractors and their subcontractors refused to deliver cargo to forward operating bases in so-called "no-go areas." The 484th was under enormous pressure to get goods to these difficult-to-reach and dangerous destinations. When too many carriers refused to run truck missions to Helmand Province, the 484th solicited white papers for an explanation. The responses were remarkably candid. One contractor wrote:

> The need to provide heavy weapons and robust security with ex pat leadership was not a requirement on the contract and now seems to be a requirement in some areas unless these missions are turned over to green security [ISAF security]. **I also believe that most involved in this contract knew that cash money is often the most effective security, but I do not think it was anticipated how high the market would drive these prices and that cash security and special security forces would so often be the only option**... RC South has been the location of nearly all of the attacks on IDIQ carriers, which needless to say presents significant challenges as it relates to controlling the quality of work and production for the [local national] drivers and security staff. **The utilization of "Green Security" will eliminate the extortion in the south; however the attacks on convoys will increase due to this fact. Some carriers are paying as much as $15,000 per truck for missions going to Dwyer and other south FOBs.**[229]

Another HNT project manager responded:

> The cost of security for these vehicles is very high and absorbs most of any profit we would make. Sub Contractors and drivers request more money to operate in this area, further adding to the problems for our companies... The cost of Private Security is exceptionally high, with companies attempting to raise their prices continually. **It is believed that a part of these charges are being paid as bribes to local Commanders, and therefore inevitably to the enemy**... As previously stated this is one of the most volatile regions of the country. There is a continuous threat of roadside IED, and ambush. There will also be a threat, not only from enemy forces but from local commanders who have not been paid their tax.[230]

Still, despite explicit warnings in formal communications about "extortion," "cash money" for security, and threats from "local commanders who have not been paid their tax," no relief was forthcoming. The contractors were pressed to run the missions regardless of the costs and regardless of their concerns about where the money went.

The Military's Request for Information on "Shakedown Money"

In September 2009, the issue briefly appeared to catch the interest of officials higher on the chain of command. On September 10, 2009, Major Koger sent an e-mail to representatives from all of the HNT contractors which asked about "protection/safe passage" payments, with the subject line "Shake down money":[231]

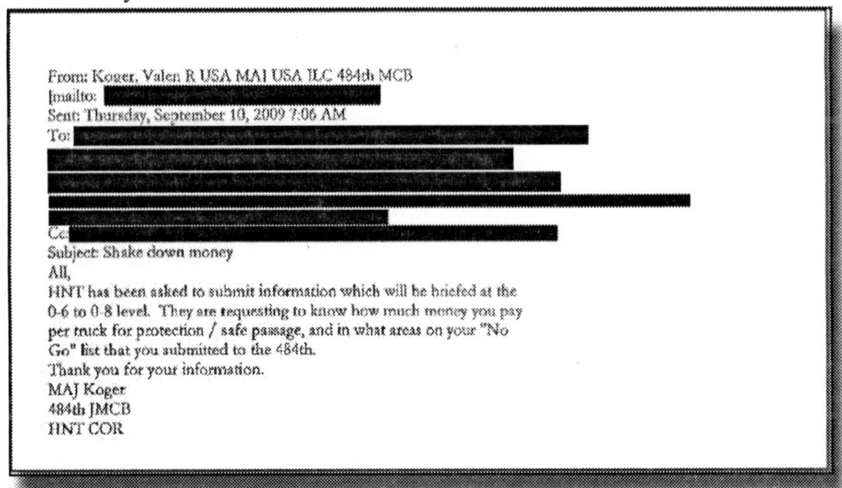

From: Koger, Valen R USA MAJ USA JLC 484th MCB
[mailto: [redacted]
Sent: Thursday, September 10, 2009 7:06 AM
To: [redacted]
Cc: [redacted]
Subject: Shake down money
All,
HNT has been asked to submit information which will be briefed at the 0-6 to 0-8 level. They are requesting to know how much money you pay per truck for protection / safe passage, and in what areas on your "No Go" list that you submitted to the 484th.
Thank you for your information.
MAJ Koger
484th JMCB
HNT COR

In Army parlance, the request for information to brief at the "0-6 to 0-8 level" refers to the rank of colonel through major general. Major Koger did not recall the e-mail or receiving any responses.[232] He speculated that someone else in the 484th had asked him to transmit the message because he frequently communicated with the contractors. He could not recall who requested the information or to whom that information was to be briefed.[233] The contractors recalled receiving the e-mail, but none apparently responded.[234]

The executives of one HNT contractor debated internally whether they should respond to Major Koger's e-mail:[235]

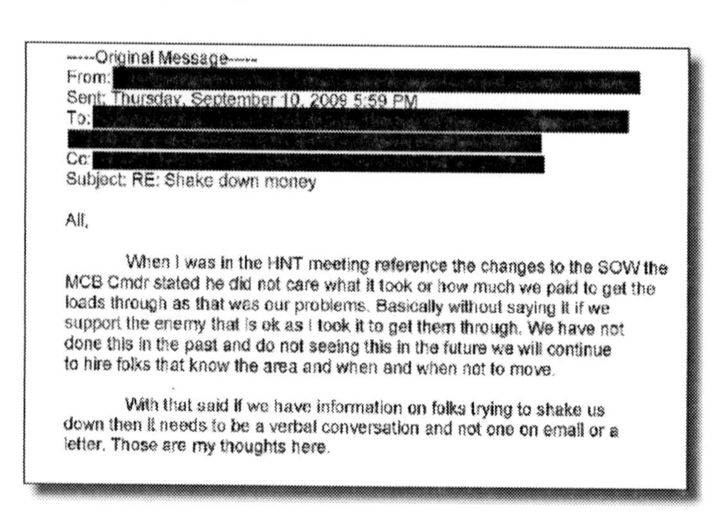

-----Original Message-----
From: [redacted]
Sent: Thursday, September 10, 2009 5:59 PM
To: [redacted]
Cc: [redacted]
Subject: RE: Shake down money

All,

When I was in the HNT meeting reference the changes to the SOW the MCB Cmdr stated he did not care what it took or how much we paid to get the loads through as that was our problems. Basically without saying it if we support the enemy that is ok as I took it to get them through. We have not done this in the past and do not seeing this in the future we will continue to hire folks that know the area and when and when not to move.

With that said if we have information on folks trying to shake us down then it needs to be a verbal conversation and not one on email or a letter. Those are my thoughts here.

While many of the contractors were willing to self-report their concerns about protection payments for safe passage orally to the HNT contract managers, and contracting officers, there is no evidence that any contractor clearly stated these concerns in writing for senior commanders.

Up the Chain of Command

The 143rd Expeditionary Sustainment Command, the 484th's higher command, was also informed of the contractors' concerns about protection payments for safe passage. Lieutenant Colonel Lewis, the HNT point person for the 143rd, stated that he heard reports from contractors that they had to pay safe passage money, or the "troll fee," as he called it, in locations in the south between Kandahar and Helmand and going up Highway 1 between Kandahar and Ghazni. He wanted to investigate what was happening on the roads but was unable to get the authorization necessary to travel to those areas because it was too dangerous. Lieutenant Colonel Lewis also said that he asked contractors to document these payments to spur further military action to correct the issue, but that he never received the hard evidence that he needed to take operational action.[236]

A contracting officer who was not present at the July 2009 contracting monthly meeting in which the contractors shared their concerns was nonetheless aware of the allegations that contractors were being extorted and paying protection fees. He stated that contractors came to him with reports of "various shakedown payments" that they had to make to the ANA, ANP, village elders, militia groups, and others.[237] The contracting officer sent an e-mail to Colonel Cottrell to share his concern: "travelling to certain FOBs requires that [the contractors] either pay a 'protection fee/toll,' hire the local elder to escort them, or take a very round about route."[238]

Further up the chain of command, one senior Department of Defense official in Afghanistan stated that there have been significant discussions within the Department of the problem of protection payments to local warlords and the Taliban, but no action has been taken: "there is no change on the horizon. We keep punting the issue down the road. It would require a major shock to the system to change the HNT business model." In his view, the contracting officers with responsibility for the contract "intentionally turn a blind eye to the problem and refuse to look past the prime [contractor] to see how the security subcontractors operate – hear no evil, see no evil, speak no evil."[239]

In response to an early story on protection payments going to insurgents, Colonel Wayne Shanks, the chief public affairs officer for ISAF, acknowledged that military officials were "aware of the allegations that procurement funds may find their way into the hands of insurgent groups, but we do not directly support or condone this activity if it is occurring." Colonel Shanks added that, "the relationships between contractors and their subcontractors, as well as between subcontractors and others in their operational communities, are not entirely transparent."[240]

The sheer size of the HNT contract and the critical importance of the supply chain did not prompt the Department of Defense to devote the necessary resources to gain visibility over the trucking operations and private security contractors. Apparently, direct allegations of payments to insurgent groups were not enough either.

Contractors Warned the Armed Contractor Oversight Directorate

In another plea for help, several representatives of one HNT contractor met with civilian and military representatives of ACOD at Camp Eggers in

September 2009.[241] In the meeting, the representatives told ACOD that it had to pay "fees" to pass through Taliban-controlled areas:[242]

4 September, 2009

Notes on Meeting with ACOD

[redacted] and I told them of the problems we have transiting Trucks into some of the more remote areas and the fact that most all of the areas are controlled by Taliban, or Tribal warlords, and we have to pay fees to transit those trucks through those areas. I had to inform them that by doing so, we would be directly supporting Afghan warlords, and Taliban that are supporting the insurgency against U.S. Forces. I argued that I was not prepared now, or at any time to assist in this bribery game to sustain warlords operating lawlessly in Afghanistan, and to do so will effectively undermine the efforts the U.S. Military in creating a stable Government able to exert its authority to these far outlying areas.

The former director of ACOD recalled having several meetings with HNT contractors where they told him that they were paying "warlords, insurgents, Taliban, ANA, ANP, everyone" for safe passage at "checkpoints" along the roads.

The country manager clearly recalled the meeting. The principal purpose for approaching ACOD was to further discuss the request for "up-arming" authority that had been raised with the 484th. The country manager told ACOD that his company had to make protection payments if it could not have up-arming authority to provide sufficient weaponry to its own security force. He recalled that ACOD was "stunned" and agreed to take this information up the chain of command.[243]

The former director of ACOD recalled having several meetings with HNT contractors where they told him that they were paying "warlords, insurgents, Taliban, ANA, ANP, everyone" for safe passage at "checkpoints" along the roads. He said that such protection payments were a common topic of concern and discussion at ACOD. He did not know anything about how the "checkpoints" might work because ACOD lacked significant visibility into the private security contractors protecting the supply chain.[244]

The former director of ACOD stated that he relayed these conversations about safe passage payments up the chain of command within U.S. Forces-Afghanistan. The former director refused to specifically identify the names of senior commanders with whom he discussed his concerns, but ACOD reports directly to the Deputy Commanding General for U.S. Forces-Afghanistan, a position held by Major General John MacDonald since February 2009. Earlier in the interview, the former director had stated that he provided Major General MacDonald with weekly updates regarding ACOD, oversight issues, and the concerns raised by contractors. The former director believed that U.S. Forces-Afghanistan had taken some steps to mitigate these protection payment issues, though he did not view the actions taken as sufficient to address the problems the contractors had identified.[245]

In December 2009, when ACOD's leadership changed, concerns regarding protection payments were still on its radar. ACOD's weekly activity report dated December 11, 2009 states that PSCs were using "illicit pay-off strategies ... for safe passage" and were funding "warl ords":[246]

DEPARTMENT OF DEFENSE
HEADQUARTERS
UNITED STATES FORCES - AFGHANISTAN
KABUL, AFGHANISTAN
APO AE 09356

USFOR-A-J4

11 December 2009

ARMED CONTRACTOR OVERSIGHT DIRECTORATE (ACOD)

SUBJECT: Weekly Activity Report Week Ending 11 Dec 09

08 Dec 09. Weekly Minister of Interior (MoI) movement meeting. ACOD discussed goal of increasing the capabilities of the ANP to the extent that PSCs will not be necessary. COL Haidary (MOI's Chief of Current Operations) agreed that increased ANP security support would benefit all and assist in eliminating corruption of PSCs. Col Le noted that another advantage of utilizing ANA/ANP was the ability to secure safe passage without interference (financially or otherwise) from warlords. COL Haidary was receptive to arranging further discussions with MOD and increasing cooperative arrangements for securing convoys.

ACOD received ANP's commitment to carve out a dedicated level of security support exclusively for Host Nations Trucking (HNT) convoys. Col Haidary informed Col Le that he has obtained approval from the Dep Minister for National Security to support HNT operations. Although with very limited capability, ANP Trans Battalion is willing to schedule a routine, pre-determined,

pre-scheduled, short duration mission for HNT. This commitment reflects ANP's view toward the corrupted actions and illicit pay-off strategies currently used by the PSCs for safe passage. ANP's cooperation illustrates MoI's pressure in working to reduce PSC operations within two years as directed by Pres Karzai. ACOD in coordination with MoI mentors and 484th members will propose a concept of operation using ANP to support HNT.

Shortly thereafter, a senior officer with ACOD requested a meeting of military officials in order "to gain systemic visibility and understand of how convoys from HNT can be transferred to [the Afghan National Army]. This is a core competency of the counterinsurgency fight against funding warlords and needs to be done asap."[247]

Both Colonel Le, the sitting Director of ACOD, and Colonel Cottrell, the PARC-A, acknowledged that they had heard reports regarding alleged protection payments and that they had no visibility into the operations of the HNT security providers.[248] They did not view this as a major cause for concern and they emphasized that the prime contractor was responsible for security, that the HNT contractors were very effective at getting critical supplies to difficult locations, and that there were few if any alternative means of delivery.[249]

Criminal Investigation into Allegations that the HNT Contract Funds Insurgents

In July 2009, two months after the start of the HNT contract, investigators from the Criminal Investigation Task Force-Afghanistan (CITF-A), working under the authority of the Army Criminal Investigation Command (CID), arranged to interview HNT contractor representatives about alleged protection payments going to the insurgency.[250]

The contractor representatives agreed that investigators were well informed about the contractors' concerns regarding protection payments for safe passage. One representative stated that he told the investigators that he was concerned that a subcontractor for his company was making protection payments to warlords and insurgents, and that the investigators asked for the names of his subcontractors.[251] Another representative said that the investigators asked him about allegations of "extortion money."[252] A representative of the same company recalled telling investigators that his company was being extorted, and if his company did not pay specific private security providers, he believed that his trucks would be attacked.[253]

These contractors stated that they never received any follow-up or heard about the results of the CITF-A investigation.[254] One contractor interviewed by investigators attempted to follow up several months later in an e-mail to the contracting officer but never received a response.[255] The investigators told Lieutenant Colonel Elwell that they were investigating contractors paying "people they shouldn't be paying... [and] unauthorized payments from contractors to people out there to not have them attack." He was unaware of any follow-up.[256]

Later in 2009, a contracting officer mentioned the investigation in an e-mail to his successor in response to an article alleging protection payments to the Taliban by HNT contractors:[257]

> You're almost done buddy, and these issues ain't on us. We had the FBI, CIA, CID and 3 or 4 other acronym agencies in the office to work this topic. You remember that one meeting were [sic] they talked to the companies "individually." ...guess nothing good came of that.[258]

A document highly relevant to this investigation has been withheld from inclusion in this chapter at the Department of Defense's request. At the time of printing, discussions regarding the origin and context of that document are ongoing.

Task Force 2010

In June 2010, Michèle Flournoy, Under Secretary of Defense for Policy, and General David Petraeus, the CENTCOM Commander, informed the Senate Armed Services Committee that General Petraeus and Admiral Mike Mullen, Chairman of the Joint Chiefs of Staff, are creating a task force to examine the impact of U.S. contracting on corruption in Afghanistan.[259] Task Force 2010 will be led by the former head of the military Joint Contracting Command in Baghdad, a two-star Navy Admiral, and will report to General McChrystal.[260] In his testimony on the subject, General Petraeus stated that:

> [Task Force 2010] will go in and augment the Contracting Command that oversees this effort in Afghanistan and then gets at who are, not only the subcontractors, but the subcontractors to the subcontractors. Literally, where is the money going, and is it all above-board, and that's a hugely important component of dealing again with corruption issues, dealing with warlordism, and a variety of other challenges that cause issues for Afghanistan.[261]

The establishment of Task Force 2010 shows that the Department of Defense is well aware, at the highest levels, of concerns that U.S. contractors are funding warlordism and corruption in Afghanistan.

IV. RECOMMENDATIONS

We cannot win a fight for hearts and minds when we outsource critical missions to unaccountable contractors.

– Then-Senator
Barack Obama[262]

As Afghanistan enters its fourth decade of war, amid rampant corruption, the country presents unprecedented challenges to the conduct of ordinary business, much less business involving dangerous military logistics operations. Throughout this investigation, the evidence shows that Department of Defense officials received a drumbeat of complaints about the HNT contract's role in corruption, warlordism, and even aid to the enemy. Unfortunately, as demonstrated in dozens of documents and interviews, a dismissive attitude about these grave allegations was prevalent throughout components of the Department of Defense responsible for the HNT contract.

There are numerous constructive changes that could be made to the U.S. military trucking effort in Afghanistan that would improve contracting integrity while mitigating corrupting influences. As the Department of Defense absorbs the findings in this chapter and considers its course of action, the Subcommittee on National Security and Foreign Affairs Majority staff makes the following recommendations:

Assume Direct Contractual Responsibility for Supply Chain Security Providers. If the United States is going to use small armies of private security contractors to defend its massive supply chain in a war zone, the Department of Defense must take direct responsibility for those contractors to ensure robust oversight. Trucking companies are wholly incapable of overseeing this scale of security operations. The U.S. government needs to have a direct line of authority and accountability over the private security companies that guard the supply chain.

Consider the Role of Afghan National Security Forces in Highway Security. To be sure, the ANP and ANA will ultimately have a role in ensuring safe passage on Afghanistan's roads. However, that would likely require a medium-term, if not long-term, transition. Numerous witnesses in this investigation have expressed extreme skepticism at any plan to rapidly transfer convoy security to the Afghan security forces due to concerns about capacity, competence, and corruption. Proposals to reform the convoy security scheme ought to take into account the Ministry of Interior's vision of a future role of Afghan security forces in highway security. If there is to be no immediate role for the ANA in convoy security, a plan must be developed to reach that goal with credible security alternatives that address immediate U.S. military logistics needs.

Inventory Actual Trucking Capacity Available to the Department of Defense. The Department should conduct a survey of the available trucking capacity in Afghanistan under the HNT contract to ensure that its needs will be met with the additional forces under orders to deploy to Afghanistan. Where there is information to suggest that there is a finite pool of trucks – some owner-operated, some as tribal assets, some owned by second- or third-tier subcontractors – adding prime contractors does not necessarily add to the pool of available trucks.

Draft Contracts to Ensure Transparency of Subcontractors. Contracts between the Department of Defense and its trucking and/or security prime contractors need to include provisions that ensure a line of sight, and accountability, between the Department of Defense and the relevant subcontractors. Such provisions should make clear the subcontractors' obligations, including full Department of Defense inspection and audit rights. Such provisions should also mandate the Department of Defense's obligation to have visibility into subcontractors critical to its wartime supply chain. There should also be robust and verifiable incident reporting requirements. Where Department of Defense regulations already require such provisions, the Department needs to enforce them.

Oversee Contracts to Ensure Contract Transparency and Performance. Similarly, the Department of Defense needs to provide the personnel and resources required to manage and oversee its trucking and security contracts in Afghanistan. These are not contracts that can be managed responsibly from a desk in Bagram or Kandahar alone. Contracts of this magnitude and of this consequence require travel 'outside the wire.' For convoys, that means having the force protection resources necessary for mobility of Department of Defense personnel to conduct periodic unannounced inspections and ride-alongs.

Analyze Effect of Coalition Contracting on Afghan Corruption. The national security components of the U.S. government, including the

Department of Defense, the Department of State, the U.S. Agency for International Development, the Department of Justice, and the Intelligence Community, need to begin to systematically track and analyze the effects of U.S., NATO, and other international donor funds on corruption in Afghanistan. Corruption is smothering the nascent efforts at Afghan governance that are fundamental to our strategy in Afghanistan. The effects of billions of dollars in development projects and security aid for Afghanistan, combined with billions of dollars spent in support of the U.S. and NATO military footprint in Afghanistan, need to be at the center of any analysis of metrics of our performance in the Afghan effort. Public reports in early June 2010 suggest that U.S. intelligence assets have been assigned to analyze Afghan corruption and governance.[263] The U.S. government needs to devote sufficient assets to the endeavor, and the mandate should include an analysis of the effects of coalition contracts.

End Notes

1 Aram Roston, *How the U.S. Funds the Taliban*, The Nation (Nov. 11, 2009).

2 Sydney J. Freedberg Jr., *Supplying the Surge in Afghanistan*, National Journal (Feb. 20, 2010).

3 *Id.*

4 Andy Oppenheimer, *Safe Passage: Managing Military Resources*, Army-Technology.com (June 3, 2010), *available at* http://www.army-technology.com/features/feature/feature86749/.

5 Sydney J. Freedberg Jr., *Supplying the Surge in Afghanistan*, National Journal (Feb. 20, 2010).

6 Adam Ellick & Salman Masood, *Six Die in Attack on Supply Rigs in Pakistan*, New York Times (June 8, 2010).

7 Andrew C. Kuchins & Thomas M. Sanderson, *The Northern Distribution Network and Afghanistan: Geopolitical Challenges and Opportunities,* Center for Strategic and International Studies (Jan. 2010).

8 Philip Pan, *Thousands Flee Ethnic Riots in Kyrgyzstan as Violence Continues to Spread*, Washington Post (June 13, 2010); *see also Crisis in Kyrgyzstan: Fuel, Contracts, and Revolution along the Afghan Supply Chain: Hearing Before the House Committee on Oversight and Government Reform Subcommittee on National Security and Foreign Affairs*, 111th Cong. (2010), *available at* http://nationalsecurity.oversight.house.gov.

9 Sydney J. Freedberg Jr., *Supplying the Surge in Afghanistan*, National Journal (Feb. 20, 2010).

10 *Id.*

11 *Id.*

12 *Id.*

13 Ann Scott Tyson, *Afghan Supply Chain a Weak Point*, Washington Post (Mar. 6, 2009).

14 Subcommittee on National Security and Foreign Affairs Staff, Interview of Lieutenant Colonel Todd Lewis (Mar. 10, 2010).

15 Sydney J. Freedberg Jr., *Supplying the Surge in Afghanistan*, National Journal (Feb. 20, 2010) (quoting Lieutenant Colonel Kirk Whitson).

16 Beth Reece, *Building Blocks,* Defense Logistics Agency, (Sept.-Oct. 2009), *available at* http://www.dla.mil/ loglines/loglinesfeature3.aspx.

[17] Sydney J. Freedberg Jr., *Supplying the Surge in Afghanistan*, National Journal (Feb. 20, 2010) (quoting Major Erik Berdy).
[18] Subcommittee on National Security and Foreign Affairs Staff Interview (Apr. 23, 2010).
[19] Subcommittee on National Security and Foreign Affairs Staff Interview (Apr. 23, 2010).
[20] W91B4N-09-D-5001 through 5008.
[21] HNT Fact Sheet provided to the Subcommittee on National Security and Foreign Affairs by the Department of Defense.
[22] *Id.*
[23] HNT Justification and Approval for Out of Scope Modification provided to the Subcommittee on National Security and Foreign Affairs by the Department of Defense.
[24] *Id.*
[25] CIA World Factbook – Afghanistan.
[26] By definition, a BPA is not actually a contract, but an agreement between, in this case, the U.S. military and a private company to allow for "a simplified method of filling anticipated repetitive needs for supplies or services." Federal Acquisition Regulations (FAR), 48 C.F.R. § 13.303-1. In contrast, an IDIQ contract is a binding contract, with a stated minimum and maximum quantity of supplies or services. FAR, 48 C.F.R. § 16.504. This difference between a BPA and an IDIQ was designed to allow the military to hold contractors accountable under the IDIQ contract for problems of the type that arose under the BPA. In reality, such accountability was absent.
[27] *See, e.g., Former U.S. Army Contracting Official Pleads Guilty to Accepting Bribes*, Department of Justice, Office of Public Affairs (Aug. 7, 2009); *Two Hawaii Soldiers Charged in $50,000 Scheme*, Associated Press (June 10, 2010).
[28] HNT Statement of Work provided to the Subcommittee on National Security and Foreign Affairs by the Department of Defense.
[29] *Id.*
[30] HNT Fact Sheet provided to the Subcommittee on National Security and Foreign Affairs by the Department of Defense.
[31] Subcommittee on National Security and Foreign Affairs Staff Interview (Mar. 5, 2010); Andy Kravetz, *Soldiers Head Out for Mission to Afghanistan*, Journal Star (Dec. 15, 2009); Subcommittee on National Security and Foreign Affairs Staff, Interview of Major Valen Koger (Mar. 18, 2010).
[32] Subcommittee on National Security and Foreign Affairs Staff Interviews (Feb. 25, 2010 & Mar. 1, 2010).
[33] Subcommittee on National Security and Foreign Affairs Staff Interview (Mar. 9, 2010).
[34] Subcommittee on National Security and Foreign Affairs Staff Interviews (Feb. 25, 2010; Feb. 25, 2010; Feb. 26, 2010; Mar. 1, 2010; Mar. 5, 2010; Mar. 9, 2010; Mar. 10, 2010; Mar. 11, 2010; Mar. 25, 2010 & Apr. 23, 2010).
[35] *See, e.g.*, Justin Blum, *Mullen Says Afghan Security Situation 'Serious,' Getting Worse*, Bloomberg (Aug. 24, 2010); *see also* Anthony Faiola, *McChrystal Urges European Allies to Show Resolve in Afghanistan*, Washington Post (Oct. 1, 2009); *see also* Craig Whitlock, *Gen. McChrystal Says Conditions in Afghanistan War Are No Longer Deteriorating*, Washington Post (Feb. 5, 2010).
[36] Renee Montagne, *In Afghanistan, Trucking Can Be a Deadly Business*, National Public Radio (Aug. 14, 2009).
[37] *Id.*
[38] Craig Whitlock, *Soaring IED Attacks in Afghanistan Stymie U.S. Counteroffensive*, Washington Post (Mar. 18, 2010).
[39] *Id.*
[40] *Id.* (quoting Lieutenant General Michael Oates).
[41] Rod Nordland, *Violence Up Sharply in Afghanistan*, New York Times (June 19, 2010).
[42] Information available from Afghan Ministry of Interior; *see generally* Moshe Schwartz, *The Department of Defense's Use of Private Security Contractors in Iraq and Afghanistan:*

Background, Analysis, and Options for Congress, Congressional Research Service, Report R40835 (Jan. 19, 2010).

[43] David Zucchino, *Afghan Civilians Soured on U.S. Security Contractors*, Chicago Tribune (Aug. 17, 2009).

[44] Moshe Schwartz, *The Department of Defense's Use of Private Security Contractors in Iraq and Afghanistan: Background, Analysis, and Options for Congress*, Congressional Research Service, Report R40835 (Jan. 19, 2010).

[45] *See, e.g.*, "Statement of Work for Armed Security Guard Services for Forward Operating Base Lightening," Department of Defense (Nov. 2009); *see also* Walter Pincus, *Contractor Hirings in Afghanistan to Emphasize Locals*, Washington Post (Dec. 7, 2009).

[46] Private Security Company Personnel Statistics provided to the Subcommittee on National Security and Foreign Affairs by the Department of Defense.

[47] *Id.*

[48] Charles A. Allen, Deputy General Counsel (International Affairs), Office of General Counsel, Department of Defense, *Memorandum re: Request to Contract for Private Security Companies in Iraq* (Jan. 10, 2006).

[49] P.L. 110-181, as amended by the National Defense Authorization Act of Fiscal Year 2009, P.L. 110-417, Section 853.

[50] Department of Defense Instruction 3020.50, *Private Security Contractors (PSCs) Operating in Contingency Operations* (July 22, 2009) (defining "contractor" as "[t]he contractor, subcontractor, grantee, or other party carrying out the covered contract.").

[51] Subcommittee on National Security and Foreign Affairs Staff, Interview of Ahmed Rateb Popal, Rashid Popal, and Commander Ruhullah (May 27, 2010).

[52] Subcommittee on National Security and Foreign Affairs Staff Interview (Apr. 23, 2010).

[53] Subcommittee on National Security and Foreign Affairs Staff, Interview of Ahmed Rateb Popal, Rashid Popal, and Commander Ruhullah (May 27, 2010).

[54] Subcommittee on National Security and Foreign Affairs Staff, Interview of Ahmed Rateb Popal, Rashid Popal, and Commander Ruhullah (May 27, 2010).

[55] *See generally* Antonio Giustozzi, *The Debate on Warlordism: the Importance of Military Legitimacy*, Crisis States Research Centre, London School of Economics (Oct. 2005).

[56] *See generally* Michael Bhatia & Mark Sedra, *Afghanistan, Arms and Conflict* (Routledge 2008) at 84.

[57] Antonio Giustozzi, *Warlords into Businessmen: the Afghan Transition 2002-2005*, Crisis States Research Centre, London School of Economics (June 2005).

[58] There is a rich and varied academic literature on the wide variety of warlords in the post-Cold War era, but there is general agreement on the following defining characteristics: A warlord controls an armed military force autonomous from the state; he has the ability to exercise violence at will; he thrives off the lack of state authority; he serves his own cause (whether financial benefit or raw power) but is not principally motivated by ideology or sectarian interests; he is not principally motivated by the aim of conquering the state or establishing an independent state. *See generally* Antonio Giustozzi, *The Debate on Warlordism: The Importance of Military Legitimacy*, Crisis State Research Centre, London School of Economics (Oct. 2005); *see also* Michael Bhatia & Mark Sedra, *Afghanistan, Arms and Conflict* (Routledge 2008) at 72-102.

[59] Michael Bhatia & Mark Sedra, *Afghanistan, Arms and Conflict* (Routledge 2008) at 229.

[60] Sam Marsden, *NATO Cracks Down on Afghanistan's Private Security Firms*, Press Association (May 13, 2010).

[61] Subcommittee on National Security and Foreign Affairs Staff, Interview of Ahmed Wali Karzai and Qayum Karzai (June 15, 2010).

[62] Document provided to the Subcommittee on National Security and Foreign Affairs by a Host Nation Trucking Contractor (redacted).

[63] Subcommittee on National Security and Foreign Affairs Staff, Interview of Ahmed Rateb Popal, Rashid Popal, and Commander Ruhullah (May 27, 2010); *see also* Aram Roston, *How the US Funds the Taliban*, The Nation (Nov. 11, 2009).
[64] Subcommittee on National Security and Foreign Affairs Staff, Interview of Ahmed Rateb Popal, Rashid Popal, and Commander Ruhullah (May 27, 2010).
[65] Subcommittee on National Security and Foreign Affairs Staff, Interview of Ahmed Rateb Popal, Rashid Popal, and Commander Ruhullah (May 27, 2010).
[66] Subcommittee on National Security and Foreign Affairs Staff, Interview of Ahmed Rateb Popal, Rashid Popal, and Commander Ruhullah (May 27, 2010).
[67] Subcommittee on National Security and Foreign Affairs Staff Interviews (Mar. 25, 2010 & May 27, 2010).
[68] Subcommittee on National Security and Foreign Affairs Staff, Interview of Ahmed Rateb Popal, Rashid Popal, and Commander Ruhullah (May 27, 2010).
[69] Subcommittee on National Security and Foreign Affairs Staff, Interview of Ahmed Rateb Popal, Rashid Popal, and Commander Ruhullah (May 27, 2010).
[70] Subcommittee on National Security and Foreign Affairs Staff, Interview of Ahmed Rateb Popal, Rashid Popal, and Commander Ruhullah (May 27, 2010).
[71] Subcommittee on National Security and Foreign Affairs Staff, Interview of Ahmed Rateb Popal and Rashid Popal (May 27, 2010).
[72] The Kandahar Security Force will be the largest PSC in Afghanistan. *See* Dion Nissenbaum, *Afghanistan War: Convoy Security Deal to Benefit Karzai's Brother*, McClatchy Newspapers (May 23, 2010).
[73] Subcommittee on National Security and Foreign Affairs Staff, Interview of Ahmed Rateb Popal, Rashid Popal, and Commander Ruhullah (May 27, 2010).
[74] Carl Forsberg & Kimberly Kagan, *Consolidating Private Security Companies in Southern Afghanistan*, Institute for the Study of War (May 28, 2010); *see also* Subcommittee of National Security and Foreign Affairs Staff, Interview with Ahmed Rateb Popal, Rashid Popal, and Commander Ruhullah (May 27, 2010).
[75] Dion Nissenbaum, *Afghanistan War: Convoy Security Deal to Benefit Karzai's Brother*, McClatchy Newspapers (May 23, 2010).
[76] Carl Forsberg, *Afghanistan Report 5: Politics and Power in Kandahar,* Institute for the Study of War (Apr. 2010).
[77] *Id.*
[78] Subcommittee on National Security and Foreign Affairs Staff, Interview of Ahmed Wali Karzai and Qayum Karzai (June 15, 2010).
[79] Subcommittee on National Security and Foreign Affairs Staff, Interview of Ahmed Rateb Popal, Rashid Popal, and Commander Ruhullah (May 27, 2010).
[80] *See* Jeremy Kelly, *Long Road to Tarin Kowt*, The Australian (Apr. 28, 2009); *see also Netherlands Pays Afghan Warlord Millions for Protection*, Radio Netherlands Worldwide (Jan. 7, 2010).
[81] Dexter Filkins, *With U.S. Aid, Warlord Builds Afghan Empire*, New York Times (June 5, 2010).
[82] Subcommittee on National Security and Foreign Affairs Staff, Interview of Ahmed Wali Karzai and Qayum Karzai (June 15, 2010).
[83] Subcommittee on National Security and Foreign Affairs Staff Interview (Apr. 23, 2010).
[84] *See* Jermey Kelly, *Long Road to Tarin Kowt*, The Australian (Apr. 28, 2009); *see also Netherlands Pays Afghan Warlord Millions for Protection*, Radio Netherlands Worldwide (Jan. 7, 2010).
[85] Gareth Porter, *US, NATO Forces Rely on Afghan Warlords for Security*, Inter Press Services (Oct. 30, 2009).
[86] *Netherlands Pays Afghan Warlord Millions for Protection*, Radio Netherlands Worldwide (Jan. 7, 2010).

[87] Christoph Reuter, *The Warlord of the Highway: Matiullah Khan is the Most Feared Crossing Guard in Afghanistan*, Vice Magazine (Nov. 2009).
[88] *Id.*
[89] *Netherlands Pays Afghan Warlord Millions for Protection*, Radio Netherlands Worldwide (Jan. 7, 2010).
[90] Mark Dodd & Jeremy Kelly, *ADF Plays Down Warlord's Role on Crucial Supply Chain*, The Australian (Apr. 28, 2009).
[91] Joshua Partlow, *Congested Border Crossing May Affect U.S. Buildup in Afghanistan*, Washington Post (Jan. 19, 2010).
[92] Meeting between NATO commanders and Members of the National Security and Foreign Affairs Subcommittee, Kandahar Airfield, Afghanistan (Jan. 31, 2010).
[93] Joshua Partlow, *Congested Border Crossing May Affect U.S. Buildup in Afghanistan*, Washington Post (Jan. 19, 2010).
[94] *Id.*
[95] Profile of *Pacha Khan Zadran*, GlobalSecurity.org, *available at* http://www.globalsecurity.org/military/world/ afghanistan/zadran.htm.
[96] *Pakistan Hands Over Afghan Rebel*, BBC (Feb. 5, 2004).
[97] *Id.*
[98] *Id.*
[99] Scott Baldauf, *Firefight Shows Strong Al Qaeda Persistence*, Christian Science Monitor (July 29, 2002).
[100] Farah Stockman, *Others Languished as Warlord Rose*, Boston Globe (Apr. 28, 2007).
[101] *Id.*
[102] *Id.*
[103] Subcommittee on National Security and Foreign Affairs Staff Interview (Apr. 23, 2010).
[104] Subcommittee on National Security and Foreign Affairs Staff Interview (Apr. 23, 2010).
[105] PowerPoint presentation (May 12, 2009) provided to the Subcommittee on National Security and Foreign Affairs by a Host Nation Trucking contractor.
[106] Subcommittee on National Security and Foreign Affairs Staff Interview (Apr. 23, 2010).
[107] Anthony Loyd, *Former Drug Lord Koka is NATO's New Poster Boy and Police Chief*, The Times (UK) (July 11, 2008).
[108] *Id.*
[109] *Id.*
[110] David Charter, Anthony Loyd & Richard Beeston, *Karzai: the British Have Made Matters Worse in Afghanistan*, The Times (UK) (Jan. 25, 2008).
[111] *Id.*
[112] *Id.*
[113] Dexter Filkins, *With U.S. Aid, Warlord Builds Afghan Empire*, New York Times (June 5, 2010).
[114] Subcommittee on National Security and Foreign Affairs Staff Interview (Mar. 9, 2010).
[115] Subcommittee on National Security and Foreign Affairs Staff Interviews (Mar. 4, 2010; Mar. 11, 2010; Mar. 31, 2010; Apr. 23, 2010 & Apr. 23, 2010).
[116] Subcommittee on National Security and Foreign Affairs Staff Interview (Apr. 23, 2010).
[117] Incident Report provided to the Subcommittee on National Security and Foreign Affairs (emphasis added).
[118] Subcommittee on National Security and Foreign Affairs Staff Interview (Mar. 11, 2010).
[119] PowerPoint presentation provided to the Subcommittee on National Security and Foreign Affairs by a Host Nation Trucking contractor (redacted).
[120] White Paper provided to the Subcommittee on National Security and Foreign Affairs by the Department of Defense and by a Host Nation Trucking contractor (redacted).
[121] E-mail (July 18, 2009) provided to the Subcommittee on National Security and Foreign Affairs by a Host Nation Trucking contractor (emphasis added).

[122] E-mail (May 4, 2009) provided to the Subcommittee on National Security and Foreign Affairs by a Host Nation Trucking contractor (emphasis added).
[123] E-mail (June 9, 2009) provided to the Subcommittee on National Security and Foreign Affairs by a Host Nation Trucking contractor (emphasis added).
[124] Subcommittee on National Security and Foreign Affairs Staff Interview (Mar. 4, 2010).
[125] Subcommittee on National Security and Foreign Affairs Staff Interview (Apr. 23, 2010).
[126] Subcommittee on National Security and Foreign Affairs Staff Interview (Mar. 10, 2010).
[127] Subcommittee on National Security and Foreign Affairs Staff Interview (Apr. 23, 2010).
[128] Meeting Notes (July 7, 2009) provided to the Subcommittee on National Security and Foreign Affairs by a Host Nation Trucking contractor (emphasis added).
[129] Incident Report provided to the Subcommittee on National Security and Foreign Affairs by a Host Nation Trucking contractor.
[130] Subcommittee on National Security and Foreign Affairs Staff, Interview of Ahmed Rateb Popal, Rashid Popal, and Commander Ruhullah (May 27, 2010).
[131] Subcommittee on National Security and Foreign Affairs Staff, Interview of Ahmed Rateb Popal, Rashid Popal, and Commander Ruhullah (May 27, 2010).
[132] Subcommittee on National Security and Foreign Affairs Staff, Interview of Ahmed Rateb Popal, Rashid Popal, and Commander Ruhullah (May 27, 2010).
[133] Subcommittee on National Security and Foreign Affairs Staff, Interview of Ahmed Wali Karzai and Qayum Karzai (June 15, 2010).
[134] *Counterinsurgency*, FM 3-24, Department of the Army (Dec. 2006).
[135] Subcommittee on National Security and Foreign Affairs Staff Interviews (Feb. 26, 2010 & Apr. 20, 2010).
[136] Subcommittee on National Security and Foreign Affairs Staff Interview (Apr. 23, 2010).
[137] Subcommittee on National Security and Foreign Affairs Staff Interview (Mar. 31, 2010).
[138] Subcommittee on National Security and Foreign Affairs Staff Interview (Mar. 5, 2010).
[139] Subcommittee on National Security and Foreign Affairs Staff Interview (Feb. 26, 2010).
[140] Testimony of the Secretary of State Hillary Clinton before the Senate Foreign Relations Committee (Dec. 3, 2009).
[141] *See, e.g.*, David Wood, *Allegation: Some Contractors in Afghanistan Paying Protection Money to Taliban*, Politics Daily (Dec. 21, 2009).
[142] Jake Sherman & Victoria DiDomenico, *The Public Cost of Private Security in Afghanistan*, Center on International Cooperation, New York University (Sept. 2009).
[143] Douglas Wissing, *How the U.S. is Attacking Taliban Funding*, GlobalPost (Jan. 20, 2010).
[144] David Wood, *Allegation: Some Contractors in Afghanistan Paying Protection Money to Taliban*, Politics Daily (Dec. 21, 2009).
[145] Douglas Wissing, *'It's a Perfect War. Everybody Makes Money'*, GlobalPost (Jan. 19, 2010).
[146] Subcommittee on National Security and Foreign Affairs Majority Staff Interview (Jan 30, 2010).
[147] Tom Coghlan, *French Troops Were Killed After Italy Hushed Up Bribes to the Taliban*, The Times of London (Oct. 15, 2009).
[148] *Id.*
[149] *Italy Denies Report it 'Paid Off' Taliban to Protect its Troops*, CNN (Oct. 15, 2009), *available at:* http://www.cnn. com/2009/WORLD/europe/ 10/ 15/italy.taliban.payments/index.html.
[150] Syed Saleem Shahzad, *The Face of Afghanistan's Resistance*, Asia Times Online (Aug. 26, 2003).
[151] Graeme Smith, *Talking to the Taliban*, Globe and Mail (Mar. 22, 2008).
[152] Jeffrey Dressler & Carl Forsberg, *The Quetta Shura Taliban in Southern Afghanistan: Organization, Operations, and Shadow Governance*, Institute for the Study of War (Dec. 21, 2009).
[153] Catherine Collins with Ashraf Ali, *Financing the Taliban: Tracing the Dollars Behind the Insurgencies in Afghanistan and Pakistan*, New America Foundation (Apr. 2010).

[154] Hayder Mili, *Afghanistan's Drug Trade and How it Funds Taliban Operations*, The Terrorism Monitor, Vol. 5: Issue 9 (May 10, 2007).

[155] Jeffrey Dressler & Carl Forsberg, *The Quetta Shura Taliban in Southern Afghanistan: Organization, Operations, and Shadow Governance*, Institute for the Study of War (Dec. 21, 2009).

[156] Dexter Filkins, *Poppies a Target in Fight Against Taliban*, New York Times (Apr. 28, 2009).

[157] Syed Irfan Ashraf, *Militancy & Black Economy*, Dawn (Mar. 22, 2009); *see also* Animesh Roul, *Gems, Timber, and Jiziya: Pakistan's Taliban Harness Resources to Fund Jihad*, Terrorism Monitor, Vol. VII: Issue 11 (Apr. 30, 2009); Catherine Collins & Ashraf Ali, *Financing the Taliban: Tracing the Dollars Behind the Insurgencies in Afghanistan and Pakistan*, New America Foundation (Apr. 2010).

[158] Yaroslav Trofimov, *Cell Carriers Bow to Taliban Threat*, Wall Street Journal (Mar. 22, 2010).

[159] *Id.*

[160] *Id.*

[161] *Id.*

[162] Subcommittee on National Security and Foreign Affairs Staff, Interview of Ahmed Rateb Popal, Rashid Popal, and Commander Ruhullah (May 27, 2010).

[163] Subcommittee on National Security and Foreign Affairs Staff, Interview of Ahmed Rateb Popal, Rashid Popal, and Commander Ruhullah (May 27, 2010).

[164] Subcommittee on National Security and Foreign Affairs Staff, Interview of Ahmed Rateb Popal, Rashid Popal, and Commander Ruhullah (May 27, 2010).

[165] Subcommittee on National Security and Foreign Affairs Staff, Interview of Ahmed Rateb Popal, Rashid Popal, and Commander Ruhullah (May 27, 2010).

[166] Subcommittee on National Security and Foreign Affairs Staff, Interview of Ahmed Rateb Popal, Rashid Popal, and Commander Ruhullah (May 27, 2010).

[167] Subcommittee on National Security and Foreign Affairs Staff, Interview of Ahmed Rateb Popal, Rashid Popal, and Commander Ruhullah (May 27, 2010).

[168] Subcommittee on National Security and Foreign Affairs Staff, Interview of Ahmed Rateb Popal, Rashid Popal, and Commander Ruhullah (May 27, 2010).

[169] Subcommittee on National Security and Foreign Affairs Staff Interview (Apr. 23, 2010).

[170] Subcommittee on National Security and Foreign Affairs Staff Interview (Apr. 23, 2010).

[171] Subcommittee on National Security and Foreign Affairs Staff, Interview of Ahmed Rateb Popal, Rashid Popal, and Commander Ruhullah (May 27, 2010).

[172] Subcommittee on National Security and Foreign Affairs Staff Interview (Mar. 5, 2010).

[173] Subcommittee on National Security and Foreign Affairs Staff Interview (Mar. 31, 2010).

[174] Subcommittee on National Security and Foreign Affairs Staff, Interview of Lieutenant Colonel Todd Lewis (Mar. 10, 2010).

[175] Subcommittee on National Security and Foreign Affairs Staff, Interview of Lieutenant Colonel David Elwell (Mar. 23, 2010).

[176] Ali Ahmad Jalali & Lester W. Grau, *The Other Side of the Mountain: Mujahideen Tactics in the Soviet-Afghan War*, United States Marine Corps Studies and Analysis Division (June 1995).

[177] Subcommittee on National Security and Foreign Affairs Majority Staff Interview (Dec. 13, 2009).

[178] General Stanley A. McChrystal, *Commander's Initial Assessment*, NATO International Security Assistance Force, Afghanistan, U.S. Forces, Afghanistan (Aug. 30, 2009); *see also* Gareth Porter, *U.S., NATO Forces Rely on Afghan Warlords for Security*, InterPress Services (Oct. 30, 2009).

[179] *See* Sebastian Abbot, *Reckless Private Security Companies Anger Afghans*, Associated Press (April 30, 2010).

[180] *Id.*

[181] Richard Norton-Taylor, *Afghan Private Security Firms 'Fuelling Corruption'*, The Guardian (May 14, 2010).
[182] Subcommittee on National Security and Foreign Affairs, Interview of Ahmed Wali Karzai and Qayum Karzai (June 15, 2010).
[183] Subcommittee on National Security and Foreign Affairs, Interview of Ahmed Rateb Popal, Rashid Popal, and Commander Ruhullah (May 27, 2010).
[184] Dexter Filkins, *With U.S. Aid, Warlord Builds Afghan Empire*, New York Times (June 5, 2010).
[185] *Id.* (quoting Hanif Atmar and discussing Matiullah Khan)
[186] Subcommittee on National Security and Foreign Affairs Staff, Interview of Lieutenant Colonel David Elwell (Mar. 23, 2010).
[187] Subcommittee on National Security and Foreign Affairs Staff, Interview of Major Valen Koger (Mar. 18, 2010).
[188] Subcommittee on National Security and Foreign Affairs Staff Interview (Apr. 20, 2010).
[189] Subcommittee on National Security and Foreign Affairs Staff Interviews (Mar 1, 2010 & Mar. 5, 2010); HNT Contract pre-award evaluations provided to the Subcommittee on National Security and Foreign Affairs by the Department of Defense.
[190] Subcommittee on National Security and Foreign Affairs Staff, Interview of Lieutenant Colonel David Elwell (Mar. 23, 2010).
[191] Subcommittee on National Security and Foreign Affairs Staff Interviews (Mar. 1, 2010 & Mar. 5, 2010).
[192] Subcommittee on National Security and Foreign Affairs Staff Interview (Mar. 9, 2010).
[193] P.L. 110-181, Sec. 862 (Jan. 28, 2008), as amended by the National Defense Authorization Act for Fiscal Year 2009, P.L. 110-417, Sec 853 (Oct. 14, 2008).
[194] Joint Contracting Command-Iraq/Afghanistan clause 952.225-0001, *Arming Requirements and Procedures for Personal Security Services Contractors and for Requests for Personal Protection* (emphasis in original).
[195] *Id.*
[196] Joint Contracting Command-Iraq/Afghanistan Interim Policy Directive #09-21 (Aug. 30 2009).
[197] Subcommittee on National Security and Foreign Affairs Staff, Interview of Lieutenant Colonel David Elwell (Mar. 23, 2010).
[198] Subcommittee on National Security and Foreign Affairs Staff Interview (Feb. 26, 2010).
[199] Subcommittee on National Security and Foreign Affairs Majority Staff, Meeting with Colonel Daniel Cottrell and Colonel Son Le (Jan. 30, 2010).
[200] Subcommittee on National Security and Foreign Affairs Staff Interview (Feb. 25, 2010).
[201] Subcommittee on National Security and Foreign Affairs Staff Interview (Mar. 11, 2010).
[202] Subcommittee on National Security and Foreign Affairs Staff Interviews (Feb. 25, 2010; Feb 25, 2010 & Mar. 11, 2010).
[203] Subcommittee on National Security and Foreign Affairs Staff Interview (Mar. 9, 2010).
[204] E-mail (Dec. 2, 2009) provided to the Subcommittee on National Security and Foreign Affairs by a Host Nation Trucking contractor.
[205] E-mail (Dec. 23, 2009) provided to the Subcommittee on National Security and Foreign Affairs by a Host Nation Trucking contractor.
[206] Subcommittee on National Security and Foreign Affairs Staff, Interview of Lieutenant Colonel Todd Lewis (Mar. 10, 2010).
[207] Subcommittee on National Security and Foreign Affairs Staff, Interview of Lieutenant Colonel David Elwell (Mar. 23, 2010).
[208] Subcommittee on National Security and Foreign Affairs Majority Staff, Meeting with Colonel Daniel Cottrell and Colonel Son Le (Jan. 30, 2010).
[209] CODEL Lynch meeting with Major General MacDonald and Staff, Kabul, Afghanistan (Jan. 31, 2010).

[210] Subcommittee on National Security and Foreign Affairs Staff Interviews (Mar. 4, 2010; Mar. 5, 2010; Mar. 9, 2010; Mar. 10, 2010 & Mar. 11, 2010).
[211] Subcommittee on National Security and Foreign Affairs Staff Interviews (Mar. 1, 2010 & Mar. 10, 2010).
[212] Memorandum provided to the Subcommittee on National Security and Foreign Affairs by a Host Nation Trucking contractor (redacted).
[213] PowerPoint Presentation (May 9, 2009) provided to the Subcommittee on National Security and Foreign Affairs by a Host Nation Trucking contractor.
[214] Subcommittee on National Security and Foreign Affairs Staff Interview (Mar. 9, 2010).
[215] Subcommittee on National Security and Foreign Affairs Staff, Interview of Major Valen Koger (Mar. 18, 2010).
[216] Subcommittee on National Security and Foreign Affairs Staff Interview (Mar. 1, 2010).
[217] Subcommittee on National Security and Foreign Affairs Staff Interviews (Mar. 4, 2010; Mar. 9, 2010 & Mar. 10, 2010).
[218] Subcommittee on National Security and Foreign Affairs Staff Interview (Mar. 10, 2010).
[219] Subcommittee on National Security and Foreign Affairs Staff Interview (Mar. 10, 2010).
[220] Meeting Notes (July 7, 2009) provided to the Subcommittee on National Security and Foreign Affairs by a Host Nation Trucking contractor (redacted).
[221] Subcommittee on National Security and Foreign Affairs Staff, Interview of Major Valen Koger (Mar. 18, 2010).
[222] Subcommittee on National Security and Foreign Affairs Staff, Interview of Lieutenant Colonel David Elwell (Mar. 23, 2010).
[223] Subcommittee on National Security and Foreign Affairs Staff, Interview of Lieutenant Colonel David Elwell (Mar. 23, 2010).
[224] Subcommittee on National Security and Foreign Affairs Staff, Interview of Lieutenant Colonel David Elwell (Mar. 23, 2010).
[225] Subcommittee on National Security and Foreign Affairs Staff, Interview of Lieutenant Colonel David Elwell (Mar. 23, 2010).
[226] Subcommittee on National Security and Foreign Affairs Staff, Interview of Lieutenant Colonel David Elwell (Mar. 23, 2010).
[227] Subcommittee on National Security and Foreign Affairs Staff Interview (Mar. 10, 2010).
[228] Subcommittee on National Security and Foreign Affairs Staff Interview (Mar. 4, 2010).
[229] White Paper provided to the Subcommittee on National Security and Foreign Affairs by a Host Nation Trucking contractor (emphasis added).
[230] E-mail (July 18, 2009) provided to the Subcommittee on National Security and Foreign Affairs by the Department of Defense (emphasis added).
[231] E-mail (Sept. 10, 2009) provided to the Subcommittee on National Security and Foreign Affairs by a Host Nation Trucking contractor (redacted).
[232] Subcommittee on National Security and Foreign Affairs Staff, Interview of Major Valen Koger (Mar. 18, 2010).
[233] Subcommittee on National Security and Foreign Affairs Staff, Interview of Major Valen Koger (Mar. 18, 2010).
[234] Subcommittee on National Security and Foreign Affairs Staff, Interview of Lavar Matthews (Feb. 25, 2010; Feb. 25, 2010 & Mar. 25, 2010).
[235] E-mail (Sept. 10, 2009) provided to the Subcommittee on National Security and Foreign Affairs by a Host Nation Trucking contractor (redacted).
[236] Subcommittee on National Security and Foreign Affairs Staff, Interview of Lieutenant Colonel Todd Lewis (Mar. 10, 2010).
[237] Subcommittee on National Security and Foreign Affairs Staff Interview (Mar. 5, 2010).
[238] E-mail (Sept. 2, 2009) provided to the Subcommittee on National Security and Foreign Affairs by the Department of Defense.
[239] Subcommittee on National Security and Foreign Affairs Majority Staff Interview (Dec. 13, 2009).

[240] Aram Roston, *How the US Funds the Taliban*, The Nation (Nov. 11, 2009).
[241] Subcommittee on National Security and Foreign Affairs Staff Interview (Mar. 4, 2010).
[242] Meeting Notes (Sept. 4, 2009) provided to the Subcommittee on National Security and Foreign Affairs by a Host Nation Trucking contractor (redacted).
[243] Subcommittee on National Security and Foreign Affairs Staff Interview (Mar. 4, 2010).
[244] Subcommittee on National Security and Foreign Affairs Staff Interview (Feb. 26, 2010).
[245] Subcommittee on National Security and Foreign Affairs Staff Interview (Feb. 26, 2010).
[246] ACOD Weekly Activity Report (Dec. 11, 09) provided to the Subcommittee on National Security and Foreign Affairs by the Department of Defense (highlight in original).
[247] E-mail (Dec. 18, 2009) provided to the Subcommittee on National Security and Foreign Affairs by the Department of Defense.
[248] Subcommittee on National Security and Foreign Affairs Majority Staff, Meeting with Colonel Daniel Cottrell and Colonel Son Le (Jan. 30, 2010).
[249] Subcommittee on National Security and Foreign Affairs Majority Staff, Meeting with Colonel Daniel Cottrell and Colonel Son Le (Jan. 30, 2010).
[250] Department of Defense written responses to questions from the Subcommittee on National Security and Foreign Affairs Majority Staff regarding the status of the investigation (May 9, 2010).
[251] Subcommittee on National Security and Foreign Affairs Staff Interview (Mar. 4, 2010).
[252] Subcommittee on National Security and Foreign Affairs Staff Interview (Feb. 25, 2010).
[253] Subcommittee on National Security and Foreign Affairs Staff Interview (Feb. 25, 2010).
[254] Subcommittee on National Security and Foreign Affairs Staff Interviews (Feb. 25, 2010; Feb. 25, 2010; Mar. 4, 2010; Mar. 10, 2010 & Mar. 11, 2010).
[255] E-mail (Nov. 17, 2009) provided to the Subcommittee on National Security and Foreign Affairs by the Department of Defense.
[256] Subcommittee on National Security and Foreign Affairs Staff, Interview of Lieutenant Colonel David Elwell (Mar. 23, 2010).
[257] Aram Roston, *How the US Army Protects Its Trucks – by Paying the Taliban*, The Guardian (Nov. 13, 2009).
[258] E-mail (Nov. 17, 2009) provided to the Subcommittee on National Security and Foreign Affairs by the Department of Defense.
[259] Testimony of Under Secretary of Defense Michèle Flournoy and General David Petraeus before the Senate Armed Services Committee (June 15, 2010 & June 16, 2010).
[260] Maria Abi-Habib & Matthew Rosenberg, *Task Force to Take On Afghan Corruption*, Wall Street Journal (June 18, 2010).
[261] Testimony of General David Petraeus before the Senate Armed Services Committee (June 16, 2010).
[262] Christine Hauser, *New Rules for Contractors are Urged by 2 Democrats*, New York Times (Oct. 4, 2007).
[263] Thom Shanker & Eric Schmitt, *U.S. Intelligence Puts New Focus on Afghan Graft*, New York Times (June 12, 2010).

In: Corruption, Contractors, and Warlords... ISBN: 978-1-61761-598-6
Editor: Jacob E. Jankowski © 2011 Nova Science Publishers, Inc.

Chapter 2

STATEMENT OF JOHN F. TIERNEY, CHAIRMAN, BEFORE THE SUBCOMMITTEE ON NATIONAL SECURITY AND FOREIGN AFFAIRS, HEARING ON "INVESTIGATION OF PROTECTION PAYMENTS FOR SAFE PASSAGE ALONG THE AFGHAN SUPPLY CHAIN"

In our constitutional democracy, Congress is charged with overseeing that the Executive Branch executes its responsibilities in accordance with law. Toward that end, this Congress has invested the Subcommittee on National Security and Foreign Affairs with a clear mandate to root out waste, fraud, and abuse, wherever we may find it.

Real oversight is a powerful tool for transparency and accountability, not for political grandstanding. Today's report by the Majority staff represents the best tradition of constructive oversight. After six months, 31 witnesses, 25,000 documents, hundreds of hours of work, and, yes, even tea with one of the warlords at the heart of the investigation, the report provides the Subcommittee, the Congress, and the American people with significant insight into how the Department of Defense has managed the supply chain for U.S. troops in Afghanistan.

An investigation of this nature is akin to a puzzle. We have laboriously gathered the pieces on the table, fit together the edges, and filled in enough sections for us to understand what the picture will look like, but there are still portions to be completed. Though the puzzle is unfinished, and important questions remain, the portrait that emerges is of the Department of Defense's systematic failure of management and oversight of contractors along the Afghan supply chain.

In the past eight years, the United States has placed an enormous burden on our brave men and women in uniform. The military has been asked to fight two grueling conflicts in some of the most difficult and hostile conditions imaginable. The challenge of supplying our troops in the field is simply staggering.

To absorb the strain of these burdens, the Department of Defense has increasingly looked to civilian contractors. In some cases, using contractors rather than military personnel makes sense. What initially was a cost-effective expediency, however, has morphed into an institutionalized reliance and a dangerous shortcut. As the Congressional Budget Office put it, the recent increase in the size and scope of contracted support in the battlefield has been "unprecedented in U.S. history." In Afghanistan today, we have roughly 90,000 troops but reportedly use almost 110,000 contractors.

As the Department of Defense has increased its reliance on contractors in conflict zones, it has not sufficiently increased its capability and expertise to manage and oversee those contractors. At the Defense Contract Management Agency, for example, the civilian workforce fell by 60% from 1990 to 2006. The combination of a massive increase in contracting and insufficient management and oversight capability is a recipe for disaster.

In the case before us today, we have just such a disaster. The Department of Defense outsourced almost all operational components of the supply chain that provides our troops with the food, water, fuel, and equipment they need to do their job. Critically, despite laws and regulations mandating strict oversight of armed private security guards in conflict areas, the Department outsourced management responsibility for these hired gunmen to other contractors.

The Department put trucking contractors, many of which only had two or three employees in theater, in charge of procurement, management, and oversight of small armies of private security contractors. The trucking companies were then directed to send their subcontracted trucks and subcontracted security through many of the most dangerous locations on Earth while carrying millions of dollars of critical supplies for our troops.

According to the report, many in the Department of Defense apparently took comfort in these arrangements. The responsibility for security and risk of loss was on the contractors and their subcontractors. The prevailing attitude was that as long as the trucks got to their destination, don't rock the boat.

When problems did arise, the response was to wrap the prime contractors on the knuckle and remind them to follow the terms of the contract.

To their credit, many of the contractors immediately recognized that they could not adequately procure, manage, or oversee mass-scale security services in Afghanistan, and they raised red flags. They told the military that they were being extorted, making massive "protection payments for safe passage," and possibly – quote – "funding the insurgency."

These extraordinary warnings fell on deaf ears. The contracting officers, contract managers, and relevant regulators consistently responded that the companies just needed to get the trucks to their destination. Contractors raised serious concerns about extortion payments funding warlords within 2 days of contract performance beginning, and yet here we are, 14 months later, and nothing has changed. I repeat: nothing has changed.

The benefits of outsourcing trucking and security on the supply chain are clear: no U.S. troops are put in harm's way and they can instead focus more of their energies on higher priority missions. This chapter helps us also weigh the costs of contracting out the supply chain.

In short, this contract has fueled warlordism, extortion, corruption, and maybe even funded the enemy. U.S. taxpayer dollars are feeding a protection racket in Afghanistan that would make Tony Soprano proud. Further consideration must now be given to determine whether the Department of Defense's failure to properly manage or oversee its supply chain logistics contracts has undermined the overall U.S. mission.

In January of this year, Major General Michael Flynn, our principal military intelligence officer in Afghanistan, wrote a public report saying that the United States is largely blind, deaf, and dumb when it comes to understanding local politics, power dynamics, and economic structures within Afghanistan. I would add that the United States is also largely blind – sometimes willfully so – to the corrupting influences of our own contracting and development work. We must be self-aware of how our massive footprint in Afghanistan can affect such a sensitive environment.

Before I close, I want to address a recurring retort to this investigation. Some say: "this is just the way things are done in Afghanistan." Others have compared the funding of warlords and possibly insurgents in Afghanistan to the "Anbar Awakening" in Iraq. There, General Petraeus used cash and other incentives to strategically co-opt insurgents. Blindly funding warlordism, extortion, and corruption in Afghanistan through multiple layers of invisible subcontracting is no "Anbar Awakening." If the Department of Defense wants to co-opt warlords, strongmen, or insurgents with U.S. taxpayer dollars, military commanders in the field need to take direct responsibility for those relationships in order to ensure absolute accountability.

The Oversight Committee is charged by Congress with stewardship of American taxpayer dollars, and with rooting out waste, fraud, and abuse, wherever we may find it. With this chapter in hand, we intend to hold the Department of Defense accountable – to the Subcommittee, to the Congress, and to the American people.

In: Corruption, Contractors, and Warlords...
Editor: Jacob E. Jankowski
ISBN: 978-1-61761-598-6
© 2011 Nova Science Publishers, Inc.

Chapter 3

OPENING STATEMENT OF LIEUTENANT GENERAL WILLIAM N. PHILLIPS, PRINCIPAL MILITARY DEPUTY, ASSISTANT SECRETARY OF THE ARMY, AND DIRECTOR, ACQUISITION CAREER MANAGEMENT, BEFORE THE SUBCOMMITTEE ON NATIONAL SECURITY AND FOREIGN AFFAIRS, HEARING ON "INVESTIGATION OF PROTECTION PAYMENTS FOR SAFE PASSAGE ALONG THE AFGHAN SUPPLY CHAIN"

Chairman Tierney – Congressman Flake – Distinguished Members of the Subcommittee on National Security and Foreign Affairs. Thank you for this opportunity to discuss the role of the United States Army in the Department of Defense's Management and Oversight of the Host Nation Trucking Contract in Afghanistan. I am pleased to represent Army leadership, the more than 40,000 members of the Army Acquisition and Contracting Workforce, and the more than one million Soldiers who have deployed to combat over the last eight and a half years and who have trusted us to provide them with materiel, supplies, and services in the right place, at the right time.

Mr. Chairman, I had the privilege of serving as the Commanding General of the Joint Contracting Command-Iraq/Afghanistan just prior to taking on my present duties and responsibilities. Although my office was in Baghdad, I traveled frequently throughout Iraq and Afghanistan. Let me state at the outset that the Host Nation Trucking contract is absolutely vital to the sustainment of our forces in Afghanistan. Contracting for, obtaining, and overseeing services in an austere environment, in a fragile economy with a poor financial system, limited rule of law, and during hostilities is a dangerous and difficult task that is being performed daily throughout Afghanistan in spite of these immense challenges.

Through the Host Nation Trucking contract, more than 90 percent of our forces in Afghanistan receive food and water, fuel, ammunition, construction materials, equipment, and other badly needed supplies. In the last year (since May 2009), there have been more than 50,000 trucking missions. Each mission is an efficient and effective means to meet the needs of our warfighters, whose numbers will increase to 90,000 when the surge is complete.

Mr. Chairman, in all Army contracting operations worldwide, we strive to be responsive to our warfighters while ensuring proper fiscal stewardship of taxpayer dollars. Our progress in these areas has been steady even though expeditionary military operations have placed extraordinary demands on the contracting system and our contracting professionals. Upholding the highest ethical standards and discipline in contracting is of paramount importance. And, even though we have confidence in the talent and professionalism of the Army's contracting workforce, we remain vigilant at all times. We are working continually throughout the Army – and actively engaged with the Department of Defense – to eliminate areas of vulnerability in contracting.

During my time with the Joint Contracting Command-Iraq/Afghanistan, I was deeply committed to maintaining high standards of ethics and discipline in all contracting operations. My team and I conducted 11 internal Procurement Management Reviews to assess strengths and weaknesses among our contracting workforce and our overall contracting operations. Through these reviews, we identified "trend forming" deficiencies and institutionalized process improvements; we provided on-site training and shared lessons learned; and we documented the results and continually improved our operations. These reviews also enabled our Principal Assistants Responsible for Contracting to allocate resources in the right places to fix areas of identified shortcomings. In addition, I conducted bi-weekly meetings with the Procurement Fraud Task Force, including representatives from the Army's Criminal Investigative Division; the Federal Bureau of Investigation; sometimes the Special Inspector General for Iraq Reconstruction; and the Defense Contract Management Agency.

Last March, another comprehensive Procurement Management Review was undertaken in Afghanistan. The final report is nearly completed, and the findings indicate strongly that contracting officers continue to maintain high ethical standards and discipline in their daily work. These positive finding are attributed, in part, to a five element training and education program that all contracting officers must complete. With your permission, Mr. Chairman, I would like to briefly outline the five elements:

(1) Defense Acquisition University ethics training must be completed prior to arriving in theater;
(2) All personnel, upon arrival, must attend a newcomer's ethics briefing;
(3) All personnel must complete the Department of Defense Standards of Conduct Office annual online ethics training program;
(4) Judge Advocates provide live ethics training twice annually at each Regional Contracting Center during Procurement Management Reviews; and
(5) The Principal Assistant Responsible for Contracting-Afghanistan sets aside a portion of every weekly meeting with Regional Contracting Center Chiefs to address ethical issues arising in theater.

Mr. Chairman, we are working constantly to improve our contracting operations and the education, training, ethics, and discipline of our contracting workforce. Our progress is significant. The Host Nation Trucking contract is a prime example. We adhered to all statutes under the Federal Acquisition Regulation for open and fair competition, while ensuring that our warfighters received badly needed materiel and supplies.

Thank you for your continued support of the outstanding men and women of the United States Army and their families. Your deep and abiding commitment to Soldiers is widely recognized throughout our ranks.

This concludes my opening remarks, Mr. Chairman. I look forward to your questions.

In: Corruption, Contractors, and Warlords... ISBN: 978-1-61761-598-6
Editor: Jacob E. Jankowski © 2011 Nova Science Publishers, Inc.

Chapter 4

TESTIMONY OF MR. GARY MOTSEK, ASSISTANT DEPUTY UNDER SECRETARY OF DEFENSE, BEFORE THE SUBCOMMITTEE ON NATIONAL SECURITY AND FOREIGN AFFAIRS, HEARING ON "INVESTIGATION OF PROTECTION PAYMENTS FOR SAFE PASSAGE ALONG THE AFGHAN SUPPLY CHAIN"

Chairman Tierney, Ranking Member Flake, and members of the Committee, thank you for the opportunity to appear before you today to discuss the program management and oversight of private security contracts.

As the Quadrennial Defense Review (QDR) acknowledged, contractors are part of the total force, providing an adaptable mix of unique skill sets, local knowledge, and flexibility that a strictly military force cannot cultivate or resource for all scenarios. Contractors provide a broad range of supplies, services, and critical logistics support in many capability areas, while reducing the military footprint and increasing the availability and readiness of resources. Typically, there is a higher reliance on contracted support during the post-conflict phases of an operation (Phase IV- Stabilization and Phase V - Enable Civil Authority).

Current operations in the U.S. Central Command (USCENTCOM) Area of Operations require Private Security Contractors (PSCs) to fulfill a variety of important security functions for the Department of Defense (DoD), the

Department of State (DoS), and other U.S. Government (USG) entities supporting Operation IRAQI FREEDOM and Operation ENDURING FREEDOM. Relief, recovery, and reconstruction of a post-conflict region are traditionally civilian functions, and thus it is entirely appropriate for civilian resources to be used to protect these activities from theft, extortion, vandalism, terrorism, and other unlawful violence. DoD contracts with PSCs to protect personnel, facilities, and activities. The roles of PSCs are analogous to civilian security guard forces, not combat forces. By using civilian resources to accomplish selected civilian tasks, military forces can focus on the military mission.

PSC personnel presently account for about 14% of the entire DoD contracted workforce in USCENTCOM, but the US PSC workforce constitutes only a minority of the total private security sector workforce protecting public, private, and international assets in theater. As of the 2nd quarter, FY 2010, USCENTCOM reported that there were approximately 11,030 armed DoD contracted PSC personnel in Iraq and approximately 16,400 armed DoD PSC personnel in Afghanistan. Table 1 below illustrates the distribution of DoD PSC personnel by nationality and delineates between the total number of PSC personnel and the number of those PSC personnel who are armed.

If contractors were not used to perform selected security functions, DoD would have no choice but to expand the number of troops required to support our increased commitment in Afghanistan. Based on rotation and dwell time models for military personnel, it would take 3 troops to replace each individual in the PSC workforce. A further complication in revising the make-up of the existing PSC personnel population is that it is not possible to draw a 1:1 correlation between US or Third Country National (TCN) PSC personnel and local national PSC personnel. Local national PSC personnel generally live off the military installation and work standard 8 hour days, whereas US and TCN PSC personnel, co-located with the military, tend to work longer shifts. Additionally, because local labor is less expensive, hiring local nationals can reduce costs for the PSCs and the Government; a difference between a salary of hundreds of dollars per month for a local national hired by the PSC versus thousands of dollars per month for a U.S. or coalition citizen hired for a similar position by the PSC, plus the costs of the housing.

DoD's requirements for PSCs to hire local nationals to perform private security functions supports the USCENTCOM Commander's counterinsurgency strategy and, according to the previous USCENTCOM Commander, has significantly enhanced force protection in the Combined Joint Operations Area. DoD's requirement for PSCs to hire local nationals creates local jobs. These local national jobs are central to DoD's counterinsurgency (COIN) operations. Contracting for local labor provides valuable connections with local and regional populations, boosts the local economy, and reduces unemployment in theater. In Afghanistan, over 90% of the DoD PSC workforce are local nationals. As such, they have assumed risk and have sacrificed to protect key movements and facilities, freeing up critical combat capability (an inherently governmental function). Table 2 below reflects the numbers of DoD PSC personnel in Afghanistan either killed in action or wounded in action as reported by the Armed Contractor Oversight Directorate.

Even as the COIN strategy is enhanced by the employment of local nationals as armed PSC personnel, security and reliability concerns must be considered. As required by statute, DoD's policies on armed PSC personnel apply to any contractor personnel at any contract tier. With impetus from senior DoD leadership, there has been a concerted effort to improve compliance with those policies. A number of significant challenges impact this effort: 1) the rapid buildup and surge of DoD forces in Afghanistan and the associated ramp up of contracted support with PSCs unfamiliar with oversight processes and procedures, 2) the lack of host nation national identity cards or any host nation federated national database of personal information, 3) a lack of reliable internet connectivity allowing timely registration in the US contractor database, 4) societal and security concerns about providing personal identification information, and 5) a culture where armed individuals are the norm and oversight, management and accountability are eschewed. DoD is working to address these challenges to facilitate compliance. For example, the Biometrics Task Force is working to determine if local biometric scans can be used in lieu of Afghan-generated identity papers, and whether these biometric scans can then be federated with existing Government biometric programs and with the U.S. contractor database.

In spite of these challenges, DoD policy requires all contractor personnel, regardless of nationality, to comply with the DoD regulations, as well as with applicable laws of the United States and of the host country. Since January 1, 2009 both Iraq and Afghanistan have exercised unambiguous national sovereignty over the operations of PSCs within their borders. In Iraq, a Stationing Agreement (SA) between the United States and the Republic of Iraq replaced the Coalition Provisional Authority Order 17 (CPA 17) that expired December 31, 2008. In Afghanistan, there is no immunity clause to protect contractors from local law. DOD continues to face challenges working with the host nation to ensure the creation of a responsive licensing regime. In both countries, USG PSCs are required to comply with host nation registration requirements and to be properly licensed to carry arms in accordance with host nation law. Further, DoD PSC personnel are subject to the Military Extraterritorial Jurisdiction Act (MEJA) and the Uniform Code of Military Justice (UCMJ) as well as local laws.

DoD PSC personnel are also required, consistent with the terms of their contracts, to obey the orders of the commander of the area in which they are operating. Violations of such orders would provide grounds for terminating a PSC's contract for cause, and may subject the individual to prosecution under the UCMJ. Finally, individual companies have their own standards of conduct and DoD contractors have demonstrated a consistent pattern of terminating the employment of individuals who violate those standards.

Table 1. Number of DoD PSCs in Iraq and Afghanistan as of 2nd Quarter 2010

	Total	U.S. Citizens	Third Country National	Local/Host Country National
Total DoD PSC Personnel in Afghanistan	16,733	140	980	15,613
Armed DoD PSC Personnel in Afghanistan	16,398	137	960	15,301
Total DoD PSCs In Iraq	11,610	1,081	9,376	1,153
Armed DoD PSC Personnel in Iraq	11,029	1,027	8,907	1,095

These numbers include most subcontractors and service contractors hired by prime contractors under DoD contracts.

Table 2. DoD PSCs in Afghanistan KIA / WIA

June 2009 – April 2010	Reconstruction	Logistics Convoys
PSC Personnel Killed in Action	81	194
PSC Personnel Wounded in Action	145	411

Table 3. DoD PSC Personnel Legal Actions (Afghanistan)

Legal Action	Number
Arrests	5
Convictions	2

To support the legal framework, DoD has instituted a broad range of management policies and operational procedures to achieve more effective oversight and coordination of PSC operations. Notwithstanding media coverage regarding incidents involving PSCs, the frequency of serious incidents by DoD PSCs is extraordinarily low. Table 3 shows the number of arrests involving DoD PSC personnel in Afghanistan and their disposition.

These numbers seem to demonstrate that, on the whole, US PSCs are operating in accordance with the host nation laws and support the overall COIN objectives. In fact, Afghan government officials have commented favorably on the performance of DoD PSCs, stating that they are, in most cases, better disciplined than members of the Afghan National Police force.

The previous Government of the Islamic Republic of Afghanistan (GIRoA) Minister of the Interior (MOI) has endorsed US efforts regarding the oversight and management of PSCs, and has indicated his recognition of the fact that as the increased troop commitment in Afghanistan progresses, the need for PSCs, with a sustained focus on expanding their hiring of local nationals, will continue to rise. The existence of these highly-trained and professional PSCs will have a long-term benefit for the Afghans, as the PSCs will represent a natural and ready source of potential police and military recruits for their governments as the use of PSCs eventually begins to be reduced. The Minister's long term focus and plan has been to accelerate development of the Afghan National Policy (ANP) as one means of eliminating the need for PSCs in five years. In other words, the MOI intends to begin to recruit current PSC personnel as part of its efforts to build, train and professionalize the ANP. I have every reason to believe the current GIRoA Minister of the Interior supports this vision.

As stated above, PSCs contracted to perform security functions for the DoD are still only a fraction of the total number of PSCs in Iraq and Afghanistan. This is one of the reasons that OSD is supporting the initiative of the Swiss Government to move beyond the Montreux Document and implement an industry-led, government-supported, international accountability regime that will apply to all PSCs in all operational environments. An industry-generated standard, recognized by the U.S. Government and other

States contracting with PSCs and incorporated into contracting tools, will be an important step towards ensuring that the operations of all USG PSCs in a contingency environment are consistent with U.S. national policy and support the long-term stability of the region in which they operate; and that PSCs under contract with other States will operate in a similar manner.

The first step in this effort is to produce a universal standard of conduct (Standard) broadly endorsed by the PSC industry. A draft of this Standard has been developed and is being refined by a working group drawn from the U.S., UK, and Swiss Governments, with equal participation from the PSC industry and non-governmental organizations active in human rights law and the law of armed conflict. The aim of the working group is to finalize the Standard and the principles for the accountability mechanism for PSCs later this year.

Looking to the future, DoD continues to analyze the factors around contract support that influence force structure and workforce mix. To assist DoD in better understanding its utilization of contract support, the Chairman of the Joint Chiefs of Staff (CJCS) established a task force to study the Department's dependence on contractor support in contingency operations. The study found that during the later stages of Operation Iraqi Freedom, the majority (80%) of contracts supported the Logistics joint capability area (JCA) while 5% supported the Protection JCA. This 5% represents about ¼ of the overall manpower undertaking security functions with the remaining ¾ being accomplished by the military. These figures are consistent with our position that PSCs are appropriately utilized for certain functions during post-conflict operations, consistent with the commander's risk and force protection assessments.

In response to a congressional mandate, the Office of Management and Budget (OMB) recently issued a public notice that provides proposed policy for determining when work must be performed by federal employees. In particular, DoD welcomes the discussion of "critical functions" introduced in the OMB draft policy letter, which are functions that, while not inherently governmental, are needed for an agency to effectively perform its mission and maintain control of its operations. This concept may pave the way for the development of a small cadre of government civilian PSCs that could be leveraged in selected circumstances. There is great potential in this area.

Hopefully, this testimony provides a documentary baseline of the topics I was asked to address at this hearing. I will be happy to answer any questions you have regarding these areas of concern and interest. Thank you.

In: Corruption, Contractors, and Warlords... ISBN: 978-1-61761-598-6
Editor: Jacob E. Jankowski © 2011 Nova Science Publishers, Inc.

Chapter 5

TESTIMONY OF BRIGADIER GENERAL JOHN W. NICHOLSON, DIRECTOR, PAKISTAN-AFGHANISTAN COORDINATION CELL, BEFORE THE SUBCOMMITTEE ON NATIONAL SECURITY AND FOREIGN AFFAIRS, HEARING ON "INVESTIGATION OF PROTECTION PAYMENTS FOR SAFE PASSAGE ALONG THE AFGHAN SUPPLY CHAIN"

Chairman Tierney, Ranking Member Flake, and members of the Committee, thank you for the opportunity to appear before you today to discuss DoD's efforts to link contracting and the flow of US government contracting funds to a winning counterinsurgency strategy in Afghanistan.

The focus of the counterinsurgency (COIN) strategy in Afghanistan is the Afghan people. We are focused on population-centric counterinsurgency operations: enabling an expanded and effective Afghan National Security Force, securing the population, and connecting the Government of Afghanistan to its people by supporting improved governance and economic development. The effects that US government contracting funds are having on the battlefield have not always contributed to the success of our strategy. Optimizing the effects of our contracting dollars in support of COIN objectives is crucial to our success.

In fiscal year 2009, the US Government spent more than $8.6 billion on contracts with a place of work in Afghanistan, of which more than $7 billion were awarded by DoD. In some cases, segments of the Afghan populace and government perceive that this money is not positively benefiting the Afghan people, and is supporting power brokers and malign actors. This is obviously not our intent nor in our strategic interest.

We intend-to-more effectively link US contracting dollars to desired operational effects and a winning COIN strategy in Afghanistan. In support of this, the Chairman of the Joint Chiefs of Staff directed the establishment of Task Force 2010, which was chartered by the Commander, US Forces - Afghanistan. Task Force 2010 will improve visibility of USG contract funding flows in Afghanistan in order to ensure that US dollars complement the COIN campaign. Improved visibility of the flow of USG contract funds will provide awareness of how money flows from contractors to subcontractors, and eventually to tribes, families and individuals.

This is no easy task. It involves an integrated effort at all levels to gain visibility of the money flow, understand and shape perceptions of the Afghan people, correct the behavior of some Afghan contractors, and gain an awareness and level of control over the second order effects of US contract spending on the environment.

Task Force 2010 will be led by RADM Kathleen Dussault, US Navy, a former commander of the Joint Contracting Command Iraq and Afghanistan. She is leading an experienced, forward deployed task force of about 25 planners, intelligence analysts, auditors, contracting experts, law enforcement personnel, and strategic communications specialists. They will integrate with other efforts in theater, including the threat finance cell and the anti-corruption task force. We have established working groups in the Pentagon to provide reach-back support to Task Force 2010 in the areas of financial intelligence, contracting policy, and COIN effects.

The vast majority of US contracting dollars in Afghanistan come from the Department of Defense, Department of State, and U.S. Agency for International Development. Task Force 2010 is focused on DoD contract spending, but will share its lessons learned with State, USAID, and other government agencies through the Special Representative for Afghanistan and Pakistan.

DoD is committed to improving the relationship between contracting-expenditures and achieving the strategic objectives that support Afghanistan's long-term success, and Task Force 2010 will make a positive difference to that end.

I will be happy to answer any questions you have regarding Task Force 2010 and its support to the counterinsurgency strategy in Afghanistan.

In: Corruption, Contractors, and Warlords... ISBN: 978-1-61761-598-6
Editor: Jacob E. Jankowski © 2011 Nova Science Publishers, Inc.

Chapter 6

Statement of Moshe Schwartz, Specialist in Defense Acquisition, Congressional Research Service, before the Subcommittee on National Security and Foreign Affairs, Hearing on "Investigation of Protection Payments for Safe Passage along the Afghan Supply Chain"

Chairman Tierney, Ranking Member Flake, distinguished members of the subcommittee, thank you for the opportunity to appear before you today to discuss the Department of Defense's use of Private Security Contractors in Afghanistan.

The Department of Defense (DOD) is just one of many entities—including other U.S. government agencies, foreign governments, international organizations, and private industry—that employ private security contractors (PSC) in Afghanistan. In recent years, the United States and many other nations and organizations, have increasingly turned to private contractors to provide security, as well as a variety of other functions, in support of stabilization and reconstruction efforts.[1] This increased reliance on contractors has fueled the growth of the private security industry worldwide.

Services Provided by Private Security Contractors

There is some debate as to what constitutes a private security contractor. Some commentators define private security as any activity that is directly related to protecting a person, place, or thing.[2] Others use a broader definition that includes such activities as providing intelligence analysis, operational coordination, and the training of military or law enforcement personnel. The National Defense Authorization Act for Fiscal Year 2008 (P.L. 110-181 Sec. 864) defines private security functions as the "guarding of personnel, facilities, or property," and any other activity for which contractors are required to "carry weapons in the performance of their duties." This definition does not include unarmed personnel providing services directly related to security, such as coordinating the movements of PSCs throughout Iraq and Afghanistan. However, many of the companies that consider themselves PSCs provide a number of services that are not considered armed security. For the purposes of this chapter, the services provided by private security contractors can be divided into two major categories: armed services and unarmed services. Armed services include

- static (site) security—protecting fixed or static sites, such as housing areas, reconstruction work sites, or government buildings;
- convoy security—protecting convoys traveling through unsecured areas;
- security escorts—protecting individuals traveling in unsecured areas; and
- personal security details—providing full-time protective security to high-ranking individuals.

For some PSCs, unarmed services represent more than 50% of their total revenue. Unarmed security services include

- operational coordination—establishing and managing command, control, and communications operations centers;
- intelligence analysis—gathering information and developing threat analysis;
- hostage negotiations; and

- security training—providing training to domestic or international security forces.[3]

PSCs Operating in Afghanistan

There are currently 52 PSCs licensed by the Afghan government to operate in Afghanistan, with some 25,000 registered security employees. PSCs operating in Afghanistan are generally limited to a cap of 500 employees and can only exceed 500 with permission from the Afghan cabinet.[4]

Many analysts believe that regulations governing PSCs are only enforced in Kabul; that outside Kabul there is little government control and local governors, chiefs of police, and politicians run their own illegal PSCs. Because of the legal restrictions placed on security companies in Afghanistan, a number of PSCs are operating without a license or are exceeding the legal limit, including security contractors working for NATO and the U.S. government.[5] Estimates of the total number of PSC employees in Afghanistan, including those that are not licensed, are as high as 70,000.[6] Responding to concerns over the actions of a number of PSCs in Afghanistan, in November 2009, President Karzai stated a goal of closing down all PSCs in two years.[7]

The Department of Defense's Use of PSCs in Afghanistan

DOD's Total Workforce in Afghanistan

According to DOD, as of March 2010, there were approximately 191,200 people working for DOD in Afghanistan.[8] This number includes over 112,000 contractors and over 79,000 U.S. uniformed personnel. Contractors made up 59% of the total workforce. 16,733 of the contractors in Afghanistan were private security contractor personnel (see **Figure 1**).

Number of Armed Security Contractor Personnel

According to DOD, of the 16,733 private security contractor personnel working for DOD in Afghanistan, 16,398 (98%) were armed. Of the armed security contractor personnel, 93% were local nationals (see **Table 1**).[9] Since December 2009, the number of armed security contractor personnel working for DOD in Afghanistan has exceeded the number of armed security contractors in Iraq.[10]

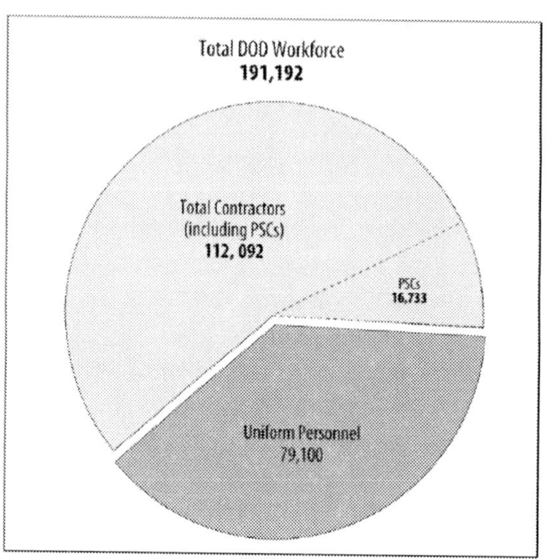

Source: DOD data.

Figure 11. DOD Workforce in Afghanistan As of March 31, 2010

Table 11. Number of DOD's Armed Security Contractor Personnel in Afghanistan by Nationality (March, 31 2010)

	Number of Americans	Number of Afghans	Number of Third-Country Nationals	Total
Armed PSC personnel	137	15,301	960	16,398
Percent of Total	1%	93%	6%	100%

Source: CENTCOM Fiscal Year 2010 2nd Quarter Contractor Census Report.

Notes: Actual numbers of employees working in Afghanistan vary widely on a daily basis due to personnel rotations, medical evacuations, and R&R travel.

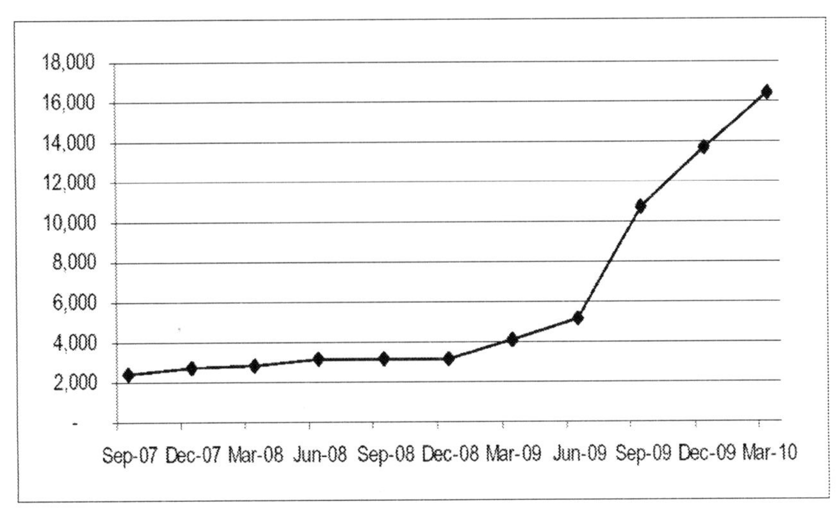

Source: CENTCOM Quarterly Contractor Census Reports, FY2008-FY2010.

Figure 2. Trend of DOD's Armed Security Contractor Personnel in Afghanistan

According to DOD, from December 2008 to March 2010, the number of armed security contractor personnel increased from 3,184 to 16,398, an increase of 415% (13,214 people) (see Figure 2). DOD attributed much of the increase in personnel to increased operational tempo and efforts to stabilize and develop new and existing forward operating bases.[11]

Armed Security Contractor Personnel Compared to Total Contractor and Troop Levels

According to DOD, from September 2007 to June 2009, the number of armed security contractor personnel increased at a slower rate than overall contractor and troop levels. However, from June 2009 to March 2010, armed security contractor personnel increased at a faster rate (217%) than total contractors (54%) or troop levels (44%). As of March 2010, armed security contractor personnel made up 15% of the total number of contractor personnel working for DOD in Afghanistan and about 9% of DOD's total workforce in Afghanistan (see Figure 3).

There are many different ways to look at this data. Some analysts could point out that armed contractor personnel make up only 9% of DOD's total workforce in Afghanistan. Others could add together the number of uniformed troops and armed private security contractor personnel and state that armed security makes up 17% of the armed force.[12] Still others could say that contractors make up 26-34% of DOD's armed security and stability force (defined as uniformed personnel and contractors who are armed to perform their core mission of conducting security operations).[13] Regardless of how one defines the role of private security contractors working for the Department of Defense, these contractors incur a risk of death and injury from insurgents in Afghanistan.

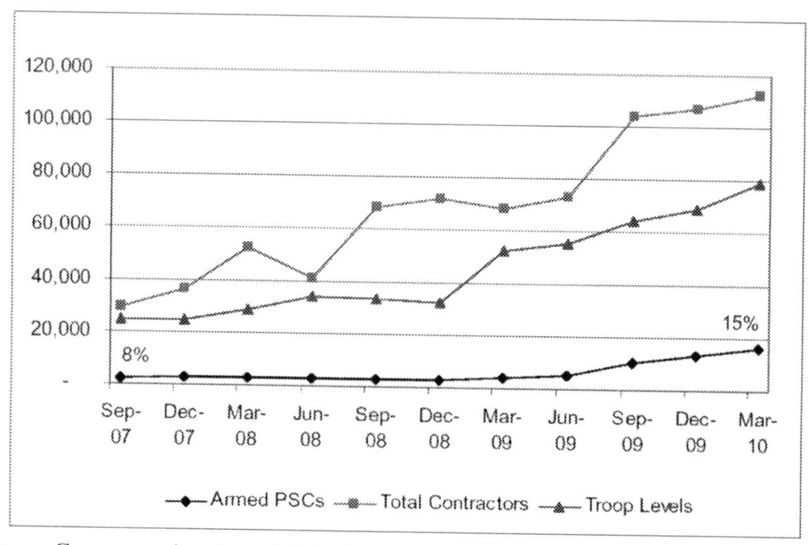

Source: Contractor data from CENTCOM Quarterly Census Reports; Troop data from CRS Report R40682, *Troop Levels in the Afghan and Iraq Wars, FY2001-FY2012: Cost and Other Potential Issues*, by Amy Belasco; see also Joint Staff, Joint Chiefs of Staff, "Boots on the Ground" monthly reports to Congress.

Notes: Percentages represent number of armed security contractor relative to total contractor personnel.

Figure 3. Number of DOD's APSC personnel vs. Total Contractor and Troop Levels in Afghanistan

Casualty Rates of PSC Personnel vs. Uniformed Personnel

According to DOD, from June 2009 to April 2010, 260 private security contractor personnel working for DOD have been killed in Afghanistan, compared to 324 U.S. troops killed over the same period.[14] Adjusting for the difference in the number of PSC personnel compared to troops, a PSC employee working for DOD in Afghanistan is 4.5 times more likely to be killed than uniformed personnel (see Figure 4).

More contractor personnel were killed providing convoy security (188 people or 72% of PSC personnel fatalities) than any other type of security, even though those providing convoy security were less than half of the total PSC workforce.[15,16]

PSCs Offer Benefits for DOD but also Pose Substantial Operational Risks

Regardless of how one analyzes the number of armed contractors working for DOD, PSCs play a critical role in U.S. efforts in Afghanistan. Yet the extent of DOD's reliance on PSCs was not planned and was executed without a clear strategy, exacerbating the risks inherent in using armed contractors on the battlefield.[17] As Secretary of Defense Roberts Gates testified, DOD's extensive reliance on contractors occurred

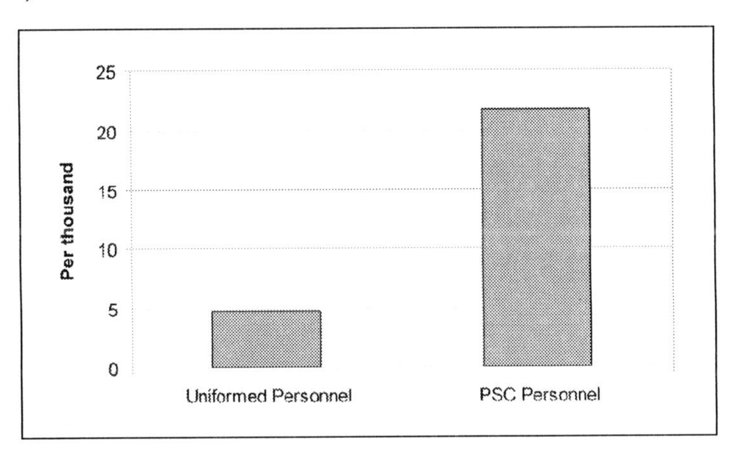

Source: CRS Analysis of DOD data.

Notes: KIA/Thousand calculated by dividing the average number of personnel deployed in Afghanistan (66,789 troops and 11,948 contractors, based on quarterly data from June 2009 to March 2010) by the total killed (from June 2009 to April 2010).

Figure 4. Number of PSC Personnel Killed vs. Uniformed Personnel (deaths per thousand)

> without any supervision or without any coherent strategy on how we were going to do it and without conscious decisions about what we will allow contractors to do and what we won't allow contractors to do... We have not thought holistically or coherently about our use of contractors, particularly when it comes to combat environments or combat training.[18]

The unprecedented extent to which DOD relies on PSCs to provide security in Iraq and Afghanistan, and the unplanned nature of this reliance, raises some fundamental questions: [19]

1. What are the benefits and risks of using PSCs in military operations?
2. To what extent should contractors be used in contingency operations?
3. What can be done to ensure that DOD improves its planning for the use of contractors in future military operations?

Benefits of Using PSCs during Contingency Operations

Private security contractors can provide significant operational benefits to the U.S. government. Contractors can often be hired and deployed faster than a similarly skilled and sized military force. Because security contractors can be hired and released quickly, using contractors can allow federal agencies to adapt more easily to changing environments around the world. In contrast, adapting the military force structure or training significant numbers of Department of State civilian personnel can take months or even years. Security contractors also serve as a force multiplier for the military, freeing up uniformed personnel to perform combat missions or providing the State Department with the necessary security capabilities when the department's civilian security force is stretched thin. In some cases, security contractors may possess unique skills that the government workforce lacks. For example, local nationals hired by U.S. government agencies working overseas may provide critical knowledge of the terrain, culture, and language of the region. In some instances, using PSCs can save the government money. Hiring contractors only as needed can be cheaper in the long run than maintaining a permanent in-house capability. According to government officials and many analysts, both DOD and the Department of State would be unable to execute their missions in Iraq and Afghanistan without the support of private security contractors.[20] According to these analysts, the risk of not using PSCs in Iraq and Afghanistan is nothing short of depriving DOD of the resources it needs to succeed in its mission.[21]

Risks of Using Armed Contractors in Contingency Operations

Given the critical role contractors are playing in supporting military operations and the billions of dollars DOD spends on contractors, the ability of DOD to manage and oversee contractors has become increasingly important. Poor contract management can lead to troops not receiving needed support and the wasteful spending of billions of dollars.[22] According to many analysts, extensively relying on private security is also undermining the credibility and effectiveness of U.S. efforts in Iraq and Afghanistan.

Can the Use of PSCs Undermine U.S. Efforts?

According to the Army Field Manual on counterinsurgency, one of the fundamental tenets of counterinsurgency operations—such as those undertaken in Iraq and Afghanistan—is to establish and maintain security while simultaneously winning the hearts and minds of the local population. Abuses by security forces, according to the manual, can be a major escalating factor in insurgencies.[23] Abuses committed by contractors, including contractors working for DOD and other U.S. agencies, can also turn public opinion in favor of anti-American insurgents.[24]

There have been published reports of local nationals being abused and mistreated by DOD contractors in such incidents as the summary shooting by a private security contractor of an Afghan who was handcuffed,[25] the shooting of Iraqi civilians,[26] and the abuse of prisoners at Abu Ghraib prison in Iraq.[27] Such incidents continue to be reported in Afghanistan. Private security contractors escorting supply convoys to coalition bases have been blamed for killing and wounding more than 30 innocent civilians during the past four years in Afghanistan's Maywand district alone, leading to at least one confrontation with U.S. forces.[28] And in May of this year, U.S. and Afghan officials reportedly stated that local Afghan security contractors protecting NATO supply convoys in Kandahar "regularly fire wildly into villages they pass, hindering coalition efforts to build local support."[29] One officer from a Stryker brigade deployed in Afghanistan was quoted as saying that these contractors "tend to squeeze the trigger first and ask questions later."[30] And unlike in Iraq, where a series of high-profile incidents involved U.S. security personnel, in Afghanistan, many of the guards causing the problems are Afghans.[31]

According to many analysts, these events have undermined the U.S. missions in Iraq and Afghanistan.[32] An official from Iraq's Interior Ministry, discussing the behavior of private security contractors, said "Iraqis do not know them as Blackwater or other PSCs but only as Americans."[33] One senior military officer in Iraq reportedly stated that the actions of armed PSCs "can turn an entire district against us."[34]

The extent to which the behavior of private security contractors in Afghanistan has hurt coalition efforts in Afghanistan was recently discussed by Major General Nick Carter (United Kingdom), International Security Assistance Force (ISAF) Afghanistan Regional Command South, who stated that the "culture of impunity" that exists around PSCs are a serious problem that needs to be dealt with and that this culture is to some degree "our own doing".[35]

Factors for Determining to What Extent PSCs Should Be Used in Contingency Operations

In 2007, then Senator Barack Obama argued "we cannot win a fight for hearts and minds when we outsource critical missions to unaccountable contractors."[36] This statement raises a critical question: is the practice of using contractors for the critical function of armed security a problem or is the problem DOD's seeming inability to properly manage contractors and hold them accountable? How this question is answered can go a long way in determining to what extent private security contractors should be used in contingency operations. To those analysts who believe that armed security should not be contracted out, possible options include increasing the size of the military, rethinking current force structure, or choosing not to engage in certain contingency operations. To those who believe that the problem is insufficient planning and poor management, the solution may be to develop an effective strategy for using PSCs, improve DOD operational planning, and enhance oversight and accountability.

Legal Issues

In January 2006, the Office of General Counsel of the Department of Defense issued a legal opinion stating that DOD may use PSCs in Iraq and Afghanistan.[37] The opinion also stated that PSCs "should not be employed in situations where the likelihood of direct participation in hostilities is high, such as military convoy security operations where the likelihood of hostile contact is high." A recent DOD instruction expanded on this issue, stating that "security is [inherently governmental] if it is performed in environments where there is such a high likelihood of hostile fire... by groups using sophisticated weapons and devices that, in the judgment of the military commander, the situation could evolve into combat.[38] The issue of whether or not PSCs are involved in combat is critical, as the DOD instruction bars PSCs from engaging in combat, which is generally defined by DOD as taking "offensive action against a hostile force."[39] As such, according to DOD and some analysts, PSCs are not engaging in combat because they are not involved in offensive action against hostile forces.

Other analysts disagree with DOD's analysis, arguing that armed security contractors are taking part in combat operations. These analysts point out that that international law makes no distinction between the offensive or defensive nature of participation in combat.[40] Some of these analysts also argue that given the frequency and sophistication of the attacks launched by hostile forces against targets protected by PSCs and the number of contractors killed and wounded in these attacks, practically speaking, contractors are engaged in combat. Last year, guidance issued by the International Committee of the Red Cross argued that direct participation in hostilities as a matter of international law included defense of legitimate military targets such as military bases, military convoys, and military personnel during an armed conflict.[41] This analysis could hold that contractors performing such services are not only directly participating in hostilities, but could themselves become legitimate targets of attack.

Management and Oversight

According to some analysts, improved oversight and accountability could mitigate the negative effects that the use of PSCs and other contractors has had on U.S. efforts in Iraq and Afghanistan, and could potentially bring the standard of behavior of PSCs in line with that of uniformed personnel.[42]

In the early years of the wars in Iraq and Afghanistan, as the number of contractors in the area of operations increased, the operational force—the service men and women in the field—increasingly relied on, interacted with, and were responsible for managing contractors.[43] Yet, a number of military commanders and service members indicated that they did not get adequate information regarding the extent of contractor support in Iraq and did not receive enough pre-deployment training to prepare them to manage or work with contractors.[44] One DOD official pointed out that the military did not have an adequate infrastructure to effectively manage and oversee contractors in Iraq.[45] And in 2007, an Army commission produced the Gansler Report, which found that Contacting Officer Representatives (CORs) responsible for managing contractors are generally drawn from combat units and receive "little, if any, training" on how to work with contractors.[46] This finding confirms what many analysts argued: that deployed military personnel were not sufficiently trained or prepared to manage contractors in an area of operations.

DOD has taken a number of steps to improve management and oversight of PSCs. In July 2009, DOD issued an instruction establishing policy and procedures for managing private security contractors during contingency operations.[47] DOD also released an interim rule modifying the Code of Federal Regulations that lays out policy regarding the use of private security contractors in war zones. The rule includes policies and procedures for selecting, training, equipping and overseeing private security contractors. DOD established Contractor Operations Cells in Iraq and in Afghanistan to coordinate the movement of PSCs,[48] and it established the Armed Contractor Oversight Division to receive serious incident reports involving PSCs and to ensure that all of the incidents are reported, tracked, and investigated.[49]

According to many analysts, DOD's efforts have improved the management, oversight, and coordination of PSCs. These and other improvements have been discussed at length and noted by the Special Inspector General for Iraq Reconstruction, (SIGIR) the Government Accountability Office, and the Commission on Wartime Contracting, which called DOD's improved management of PSCs in Iraq a "success story".[50] Many analysts believe that such improvements can help rein in contractor behavior that undermines U.S. efforts.

Recognizing the improvements that have been made to date, most analysts maintain that gaps still remain in DOD's management of PSCs.[51] For example, in its April 2010 report to Congress, SIGIR stated that it "continues to make recommendations" on how DOD can make better use of PSCs in contingency reconstruction operations.[52] DOD officials acknowledge that the management of PSCs is a work in progress that still has a way to go.

Ensuring that DOD Sufficiently Plans for the Use of Contractors in Future Military Operations

The extent to which DOD plans for the use of contractors in the future can help ensure that DOD puts a more effective management system in place. Such planning could also ensure that contractors are used as a way to improve overall operational effectiveness and not primarily because DOD unexpectedly has insufficient military personnel to perform critical functions.

In 2003, GAO issued a report entitled *Military Operations: Contractors Provide Vital Services to Deployed Forces but Are Not Adequately Addressed in DOD Plans.* [53] In the report, GAO found that the U.S. operational plans for the war in Iraq contained only limited information on contractor support even though DOD was aware of the need to identify contractors providing essential services as early as 1988. This same opinion was expressed in 2008 by a U.S. colonel in Baghdad who was responsible for overseeing PSCs in Iraq. In explaining all of the progress being made by DOD in improving its management of PSCs, he stated that the question is not what DOD is doing to fix the problem now; rather, he said the real question is why DOD was not thinking about this issue ten years ago when steps could have been taken to avoid the situation that we are in today.[54]

This raises another question: namely, to what extent is DOD actively assessing when and to what extent armed security contractors, and even contractors in general, should be used in future military operations. A number of analysts believe that DOD has not sufficiently engaged in such an assessment. This belief is in line with a recently released GAO report entitled *Warfighter Support: DOD Needs to Improve Its Planning for Using Contractors to Support Military Operations.*[55] Earlier this year, General Stanley McChrystal reportedly addressed this issue when he stated that the U.S. has created a dependency on contractors that "is greater than it ought to be."[56]

Some analysts argue that DOD missed an opportunity to address the issue in the 2010 Quadrennial Defense Review (QDR). The QDR has a seven page section on counterinsurgency, stability, and counterterrorism operations, including a list of ten priorities for improvement. These analysts point out that the word "contractor" does not appear once in the discussion, despite the fact that contractors make up more that 60% of DOD's workforce in Afghanistan, including more than 13,000 armed contractors.

Despite not being included in the QDR, senior DOD officials have begun to examine the extent to which DOD relies on contactors, including PSCs. In December 2008, Acting Chairman of the Joint Chiefs of Staff, General James E. Cartwright, established the Dependence on Contractor Support in Contingency Operations Task Force. This task force was charged with determining the extent to which DOD relies on contractors, and to use this analysis to consider how to use contractors in contingency operations as well as help plan DOD's future force structure. The task force conducted a detailed study of contractors in Iraq and has briefed the most senior levels of the Department of Defense. A number of analysts believe that this effort is a step in the right direction.

Incorporating the Role of Contractors into Military Education and Exercises

A number of experts have argued that increased training and education in managing contractors during contingency operations is necessary for non-acquisition personnel throughout the military. The Gansler Report stated that the Army needs to train operational commanders on the important role contracting plays in warfighting, as well as on their responsibilities in the process. The report called for adding courses on contractors in expeditionary operations into the curricula of the services' professional military education programs.[57] Echoing the Gansler Report, an official at the U.S. Army Materiel Command wrote that "Contractor logistics support must be integrated into doctrine and taught at every level of professional schooling in each component."[58] The calls for more robust training are not new. For example, in 2003, GAO testified before the House Armed Services Committee, Subcommittee on Readiness, stating "Without training, many commanders, senior military personnel, and contracting officers' representatives are not aware of their roles and responsibilities in dealing with contractors."[59]

Some analysts argue that education is not enough: that to truly integrate contractors into the culture of the military, it is critical to incorporate contractors and contract operations in military exercises. According to these analysts, only through military exercises will military planners and operational commanders truly understand the role of and how to manage contractors during military operations.

Mr. Chairman, distinguished members of the subcommittee, this concludes my testimony. Thank you again for the opportunity to appear before you to discuss these issues. I will be pleased to respond to any questions you might have.

End Notes

[1]According to one report, "Not since the 17th century has there been such a reliance on private military actors to accomplish tasks directly affecting the success of military engagements." Fred Schreier and Marina Caparini. *Privatising Security: Law, Practice and Governance of Private Military and Security Companies*. Geneva, Switzerland: Geneva Centre for the Democratic Control of Armed Forces, March 2005. p. 1. For discussions on the growth of private companies providing security and other support to military efforts worldwide, see, for example: Deborah D. Avant. *The Market for Force: The Consequences of Privatizing Security*. Cambridge, UK; New York: Cambridge University Press, 2005; Simon Chesterman and Chia Lehnardt. *From Mercenaries to Market: The Rise and Regulation of Private Military Companies*. Oxford, UK; New York: Oxford University Press, 2007; and Singer, Peter W. *Corporate Warriors: The Rise of the Privatized Military Industry*. Ithaca, NY: Cornell University Press, 2003. For a discussion of United Nations use of such contractors, see William J. Durch and Tobias C. Berkman. *Who Should Keep the Peace? Providing Security for the Twenty-First-Century Peace Operations*. Washington, D.C.: The Henry L. Stimson Center, September 2006. pp. 83-84.

[2] Doug Brooks, President of the International Peace Operations Association, an industry trade group, defines private security as any activity directly related to protecting a "noun."

[3] Contractors providing weapons training may be armed. However, the use of weapons for training purposes is categorized here as an unarmed service because the weapons are used as training tools and not to provide armed security.

[4] Based on discussions and emails with S. J. A. Brooking, Advisor to the Minister of Interior, Afghanistan, November 19, 2009. Some of the companies that had more than 500 employees prior to the cap taking effect were grandfathered in and permitted to maintain a larger force.

[5] Based on DOD documentation and on official in Afghanistan. See also CRS Report R40835, The Department of Defense's Use of Private Security Contractors in Iraq and Afghanistan: Background, Analysis, and Options for Congress, by Moshe Schwartz.

[6] The majority of PSC personnel working in Afghanistan do not work for the U.S. government. David Zucchino, "Private security forces unnerve Afghans," *Chicago Tribune*, August 17, 2009.

[7] Kathy Gannon and Elena Becastoros, "Karzai makes big promises at inaugural," *Desert Morning News (based on Associated Press story)*, November 20, 2009, pp. A-04; John Boone, "The agenda: Five-year timetable for Afghan troops to replace foreign forces," *The Guardian*, November 20, 2009, p. International: 29.

[8] For purposes of this testimony, DOD's workforce is defined as uniformed personnel and the contractor workforce. DOD civilian personnel are excluded from this count. According to DOD's *Joint Personnel Status Report*, as of September 8, 2009, the DOD civilian workforce in Afghanistan was 1,706 employees (1.0% of the total force).

[9] According to DOD, since September 2007, local nationals have made up 90% or more of all armed security contractors in Afghanistan.

[10] As of December 31, 2009 there were 13,717 armed private security personnel in Afghanistan compared to 9,431 in Iraq. As of March 31, 2010 there were 16,398 armed private security personnel in Afghanistan compared to 11,029 in Iraq.

[11] CENTCOM FY2009 4th Quarter and FY2010 2nd Quarter Contractor Census.

[12] See CRS Report R40835, *The Department of Defense's Use of Private Security Contractors in Iraq and Afghanistan: Background, Analysis, and Options for Congress*, by Moshe Schwartz.

[13] Ibid.

[14] PSC data provided by DOD to CRS on May 7, 2010. Troop data can be found at http://siadapp.dmdc.osd.mil/personnel/CASUALTY/oef_list_of_names.xls, *Operation Enduring Freedom—Names, Alphabetical Order*.

[15] Based on data provided by DOD on May 7, 2010.

[16] Based on DOD documents and discussions with DOD officials.

[17] U.S. Government Accountability Office, *Military Operations: Implementation of Existing Guidance and Other Actions Needed to Improve DOD's Oversight and Management of Contractors in Future Operations*, GAO-08-436T, January 28, 2008, p. 6. See also U.S. Government Accountability Office, *Defense Management: DOD Needs to Reexamine Its Extensive Reliance on Contractors and Continue to Improve Management and Oversight*, GAO-08-572T, March 11, 2008, p. 14.

[18] U.S. Congress, Senate Committee on Armed Services, *To Receive Testimony on the Challenges Facing the Department of Defense*, 110th Cong., 2nd sess., January 27, 2009.

[19] Iraq and Afghanistan appear to be the first two instances where the U.S. government has used private contractors extensively for protecting persons and property in combat or stability operations where host country security forces are absent or deficient, but it is not the first time private contractors have been used for such purposes. The U.S. Government Accountability Office (GAO) reported that contractors have provided security guards in the Balkans and Southwest Asia. *Military Operations: Contractors Provide Vital Services to Deployed Forces but Are Not Adequately Addressed in DOD Plans*. GAO-03-695, June 2003, p 8. The United States also uses contractors (U.S. and foreign citizens) for guard duty at U.S. military installations and U.S. embassies and consulates in a number of countries where stability generally is not an issue.

[20] CRS Report MM70119, *Private Security Contractors: Possible Legislative Approaches. Online Video. DVD.*, coordinated by Kennon H. Nakamura.

[21] CRS Report MM70119, *Private Security Contractors: Possible Legislative Approaches. Online Video. DVD.*, coordinated by Kennon H. Nakamura.

[22] U.S. Government Accountability Office. *Stabilizing And Rebuilding Iraq: Actions Needed to Address Inadequate Accountability over U.S. Efforts and Investments*. GAO-08-568T. March 11, 2008. p. 4,6; See also Urgent Reform Required: Army Expeditionary Contracting, op. cit., p. 2.

[23] Department of Defense, *Counterinsurgency*, FM 3-24, December 2006, p. 1-9

[24] Chairman of the Joint Chiefs of Staff, *Operational Contract Support*, Joint Publication 4-10, October 17, 2008, pp. IV-20; See also *Counterinsurgency*, p. 1-9. *Operational Contract Support* recognizes that local nationals may not always draw a distinction between government contractors and the U.S. military.

[25] Bruce Alpert, "Killing in Afghanistan hits very close to home; N.O. man is accused of cold-blooded crime," *Times-Picayune*, December 17, 2008, p. 1.

[26] Mark Townsend, "National: Iraq victims sue UK security firm: Guards employed by Hampshire-based company are," *The Observer*, January 11, 2009, p. 14.

[27] Department of Defense, Investigation of Intelligence Activities at Abu Ghraib, August 23, 2004. See http://oai.dtic.mil/oai/oai?verb=getRecord&metadataPrefix=html&identifier=ADA429125.

The contractors involved in the Abu Ghraib incident are generally considered not to have been private security contractors.

[28] Sean Taylor, "Trigger-Happy Security Complicates Convoys ," *Army Times*, December 1, 2009.

[29] Sebastian Abbot, "Private Guards Anger U.S., Afghans," *Associated Press*, May 1, 2010.

[30] Ibid.

[31] Sean Taylor, "Trigger-Happy Security Complicates Convoys ," *Army Times*, December 1, 2009; Sebastian Abbot, "Wild and Reckless Behavior," *The Associated Press*, May 1, 2010; "Afghanistan Bars Security Firms After Civilian Deaths," *Agence France Presse*, May 9, 2010; Noor Kahn, "Karzai: Afghan guards employed by US killed police," *AP Newswire*, June 29, 2009.

[32] See David Zucchino, "Private security forces unnerve Afghans," *Chicago Tribune*, August 17, 2009; Sebastian Abbot, "Wildand Reckless Behavior," *The Associated Press*, May 1, 2010; "Afghanistan Bars Security Firms After Civilian Deaths," *Agence France Presse*, May 9, 2010.

[33] Steve Fainaru, "Where Military Rules Don't Apply; Blackwater's Security Force in Iraq Given Wide Latitude by State Department," *Washington Post*, September 20, 2007, Pg. A1.

[34] Anna Mulrine and Keith Whitelaw, "Private Security Contractors Face Incoming Political Fire," *U.S. News & World Report*, October 5, 2007.

[35] "Major General Nick Carter (U.K. Royal Army) Holds a Defense Department News Briefing Via Teleconference From Afghanistan," CQ Transcript, May 26, 2010.

[36] Hauser, C., *New Rules for Contractors are Urged by 2 Democrats*, the New York Times, October 4, 2007.

[37] Charles A. Allen, Deputy General Counsel, *Request to Contract for Private Security Companies in Iraq*, Department of Defense Office of General Counsel, Memorandum, January 10, 2006, p. 4.

[38] Dr. Clifford L. Stanley, Undersecretary of Defense for Personnel and Readiness, *Policy and Procedures for Determining Workforce Mix*, Department of Defense, Instruction 1100.22, April 12, 2010, p. 19.

[39] Ibid.

[40] Even according to analysts who believe that armed contractors are engaging in combat, there are significant differences between contractors and uniformed personnel. For example, contractors are bound by the terms of the contract, do not fall within the same chain of command as uniformed personnel, and are barred by contract and DOD regulations from participating in offensive activities. For a more detailed discussion on whether armed security contractors are engaging in combat, see CRS Report R40991, *Private Security Contractors in Iraq and Afghanistan: Legal Issues*, by Jennifer K. Elsea.

[41] Nilz Melzer, Interpretive Guidance on the Notion of Direct Participation in Hostilities Under International Humanitarian Law, International Committee of the Red Cross, Geneva, Switzerland, May 2009, p. 38.

[42] According to an Army investigative report, a lack of good contractor oversight at Abu Ghraib prison contributed to fostering a permissive environment in which prisoner abuses took place at the hands of contractors. Department of Defense, Investigation of Intelligence Activities at Abu Ghraib, August 23, 2004, p. 52. The report found "Proper oversight did not occur at Abu Ghraib due to a lack of training and inadequate contract management ... [T]his lack of monitoring was a contributing factor to the problems that were experienced with the performance of the contractors at Abu Ghraib." See http://oai.dtic.mil/oai/oai?verb=getRecord&metadataPrefix=html&identifier=ADA429125.

[43] The operational force, including servicemen and women conducting military operations on the battlefield, consists of those forces that "conduct full spectrum operations around the world." The institutional force, including acquisition personnel, supports the operational force. "Institutional organizations provide the infrastructure necessary to raise, train, equip,

deploy and ensure the readiness of' military forces. See *Urgent Reform Required: Army Expeditionary Contracting*, op. cit. p. 1.

[44] U.S. Government Accountability Office. *DOD Needs to Reexamine Its Extensive Reliance on Contractors and Continue to Improve Management and Oversight*. GAO-08-572T. Highlights page. March 11, 2008; Also based on discussions with military personnel deployed in Iraq.

[45] Kathryn T.H. Syzmanski, Command Counsel U.S. Army Materiel Command in Atlanta on August 9, 2004. American Bar Association Section of Public Contract Law, *Contractors on the Battlefield: Exploration of Unique Liability and Human Relations Issues*, Volume II.

[46] Commission on Army Acquisition and Program Management in Expeditionary Operations. *Urgent Reform Required: Army Expeditionary Contracting*. October 31, 2007. p. 43.

[47] Ashton Carter, *Private Security Contractors (PSCs) Operating in Contingency Operations*, Department of Defense, Acquisition, Technology, and Logistics, DODI 3020.50, July 22, 2009.

[48] The Armed Contractor Oversight Division in Iraq was renamed the Armed Contractor Oversight Bureau. For a detailed discussion on DOD efforts to improve the coordination of PSC movements throughout Iraq, see Government Accountability Office, *Rebuilding Iraq: DOD and State Department Have Improved Oversight and Coordination of Private Security Contractors in Iraq, but Further Actions Are Needed to Sustain Improvements*, GAO-08-966, July 31, 2008; Special Inspector General for Iraq Reconstruction, *Field Commanders See Improvements in Controlling and Coordinating Private Security Contractor Missions in Iraq*, SIGIR 09-022, July 28, 2009.

[49] Special Inspector General for Iraq Reconstruction, Investigation and Remediation Records Concerning Incidents of Weapons Discharges by Private Security Contractors Can Be Improved, SIGIR 09-023, July 28, 2009.

[50] Ibid. See also, U.S. Congress, House Committee on Oversight and Government Reform, Subcommittee on National Security and Foreign Affairs, *Commission on Wartime Contracting: Interim Findings and Path Forward*, 111th Cong., 1st sess., June 10, 2009.

[51] U.S. Government Accountability Office, Contingency Contract Management: DOD Needs to Develop and Finalize Background and Other Standards for Private Security Contactors, GAO-09-351, July 31, 2009.

[52] Special Inspector General for Iraq Reconstruction, *Quarterly Report to the United States Congress*, April 30, 2010, p. 100.

[53] U.S. General Accounting Office, Military Operations: Contractors Provide Vital Services to Deployed Forces but Are Not Adequately Addressed in DOD Plans, GAO-03-695, June 24, 2003, p. 2.

[54] Based on in-person conversation in Baghdad, March 2008.

[55] U.S. Government Accountability Office, Warfighter Support: DOD Needs to Improve Its Planning for Using Contractors to Support Military Operations, GAO-10-472, March 30, 2010.

[56] "Too Many Contractors in Afghanistan - McCrystal," *Trend News Agency*, April 17, 2010.

[57] Urgent Reform Required: Army Expeditionary Contracting, op. cit., p. 7.

[58] Contractors on the Battlefield Volume II, op. cit.

[59] U.S. Government Accountability Office. Military Operations: Contractors Provide Vital Services to Deployed Forces but Are Not Adequately Addressed in DOD Plans, GAO-03-695, June 2003. p. 36.

In: Corruption, Contractors, and Warlords... ISBN: 978-1-61761-598-6
Editor: Jacob E. Jankowski © 2011 Nova Science Publishers, Inc.

Chapter 7

TESTIMONY OF CARL FORSBERG, INSTITUTE FOR THE STUDY OF WAR, BEFORE THE SUBCOMMITTEE ON NATIONAL SECURITY AND FOREIGN AFFAIRS, HEARING ON "PRIVATE SECURITY CONTRACTING AND THE COUNTERINSURGENCY MISSION IN AFGHANISTAN"

RECOMMENDATIONS

- A strong personality-driven political order is emerging in Afghanistan which undermines ISAF's goals. This chapter discusses the historical context of governance structures in Kandahar, the declining influence of tribes, Kandahar's current powerbrokers, and the rise of the Karzai family.
- Kandahar is strategic terrain for the Quetta Shura Taliban and the Karzai family, and a central focus of ISAF's 2010 counterinsurgency campaign.
- Ahmed Wali Karzai's influence over Kandahar is the central obstacle to any of ISAF's governance objectives, and a consistent policy for dealing with him must be a central element of any new strategy. Wali Karzai's behavior and waning popularity among local populations promote instability and provide space for the Taliban to exist.

- ISAF has inadvertently strengthened the forces that undermine legitimate government institutions. ISAF must shape the political landscape in Kandahar so that the local government becomes a credible partner.
- ISAF must develop a new coherent strategy that is unified in both Kandahar and Kabul and that recognizes the means by which informal power structures co-opt and undermine the development of robust institutions.
- A new ISAF strategy must include:
    - Unity of effort among coalition actors at the national and provincial levels.
    - Comprehensive intelligence on the interests and relationships of local powerbrokers, contracting networks, and on the connections between Kabul and Kandahar.
    - Reform of ISAF contracting, to ensure distribution of ISAF funding to a broad range of constituencies, and to ensure that contracts do not create strong military-commercials networks.
    - Disarmament and demobilization of private security forces and private militias.
    - Building ministerial capacity in Kandahar and Kabul to ensure strong and independent security forces.

KEY FINDINGS

- While most actors in Kandahar call themselves tribal leaders, few influential actors in Kandahar derive their influence from this position. Control over guns, money, and foreign support have become more important as sources of power.
    - Influential actors in Kandahar nevertheless attempt to maintain influence over the tribal system and often organize their networks, militias, and cartels along tribal lines.
- The Karzai family is the key to politics in Kandahar. The Karzai family and the Quetta Shura Taliban have emerged as the most powerful forces.
    - Since 2001, Ahmed Wali Karzai has gradually built a powerful empire in Kandahar through the support of foreign backers and by

bringing under his influence the province's key commercial, military, and contracting networks.

- The Karzai family's leading members, Hamid, Mahmoud, Qayum, and Ahmed Wali, have built significant influence in different spheres, strengthening the family's power as a whole.
- President Hamid Karzai reassigned Kandahar Governor Gul Agha Sherzai to Nangahar province in 2005, replacing him with Asadullah Khalid, a family ally. This gave Ahmed Wali Karzai informal control of the province.

- Kandahar's political and economic life is dominated by several commercial and military networks.
    - Ahmed Wali Karzai is at the center of a number of these networks, and has considerable influence over business life in Kanahar City itself, with significant private security, real estate, and contracting interests.
    - His control of private security forces, as well as his influence over contracting firms like Watan Risk Management and Asia Security Group allows him to enforce his political will in the city and exert influence over all business transactions.
    - Ahmed Wali Karzai has formed alliances with other key strongmen in Kandahar, who control transit routes and run commercial/military networks. These strongmen include Arif Noorzai, Abdul Razak, and Matiullah Khan.
    - Family members and allies of Gul Agha Sherzai run a rival commercial network to Ahmed Wali Karzai's.
- Ahmed Wali Karzai has used his informal power and his connections to the Afghan state to give him shadow ownership of the government of Kandahar.
    - Through the Independent Directorate of Local Governance, the Karzai administration in Kabul controls the appointment of provincial governors and district officials, giving it considerable power over local government.
    - Given Ahmed Wali Karzai's influence in Kabul, local government officials understand that challenging Ahmed Wali Karzai's influence would jeopardize their political futures.
    - Local powerbrokers have intentionally kept the official police force weak. This allows them to manipulate the police force to their ends and forces ISAF to rely on their private security companies. Because many of these companies are controlled by

or allied with Ahmed Wali Karzai, this ensures both revenue and influence.

- The local population sees the government as an exclusive oligarchy devoted to its own enrichment and closely tied to the international coalition.
  - Anti-government sentiments are exploited and aggravated by the Taliban. Many of the local powerbrokers who are excluded from Wali Karzai's network see the Taliban insurgency as the only viable means of political opposition.
  - The 2009 presidential and provincial council elections demonstrated that Ahmed Wali Karzai's popular base in Kandahar was narrowing.
- Despite limited popular support, Ahmed Wali Karzai's maintenance of power rests on three interdependent pillars. These are:
  - That the international coalition, despite growing frustrations, will continue to give him de facto support where it matters and will not take actions that challenge his fundamental interests.
  - That he will continue to receive critical state backing and continue to control the formal government of Kandahar. He assumes that Hamid Karzai will continue to support him and that the government ministries in Kabul will not challenge his influence due to his brother's political ascendancy.
  - That he will maintain the ability to exert power over locals through his use of force and his control over the provincial economy.

Consolidating Private Security Companies in Southern Afghanistan

Dozens of Private Security Companies (PSCs) operate in Kandahar city and province, frequently doubling as the militias of local powerbrokers. These armed groups also operate on a contractual basis to provide security for the International Security Assistance Force (ISAF) and private, Afghan companies. Because PSCs are under the control of powerful individuals, rather than the Afghan National Security Forces, they compete with state security forces and interfere with a government monopoly on the use of force. There is growing pressure from ISAF and within the Afghan government to reform and regulate these companies. Major General Nick Carter, the commander of Regional Command-South (RC-S), recently briefed that ISAF was developing a strategy to regulate PSCs as part of the Kandahar Operations unfolding in summer 2010.[1]

If not properly structured, however, the regulation of these PSCs in Kandahar may reinforce the existing power structures, strengthen the hand of local powerbrokers such as Ahmed Wali Karzai, and further weaken the ANSF. An initiative underway to consolidate the security companies in southern Afghanistan is likely to exacerbate the problems caused by PSCs, rather than reducing their influence.

Security Companies Now in Kandahar

The Ministry of Interior (MOI) regulations of private security companies forbid senior officials, such as the President and Cabinet Ministers, and their immediate family members from directly controlling PSCs.[2] Some of the PSCs, consequently, are owned by relatives twice removed from these senior officials, in accordance with the law. Hence, Ahmad and Rashid Popal, two cousins of President Karzai own Watan Risk Management, a large PSC operating in Afghanistan, and another cousin, Hashmat Karzai, runs Asia Security Group, another major PSC.[3]

Although there are numerous private security companies in Kandahar, they are ultimately controlled or influenced by a small number of powerbrokers. Ahmad Wali Karzai retains significant influence with the PSCs run by the Karzai family, including Asia Security Group and Watan Risk Management. He also directly controls other forces, including his own personal security detail and the Kandahar Strike Force.[4] Finally, his hand-picked commanders, Haji Seyid Jan Khakrezwal and Akhtar Mohammad, respectively control the Provincial Council Security Force and the security forces that operate in Ayno Mena, the gated community in Kandahar that he financed and developed.[5] Finally, Watan Risk Management has subcontracted to the security forces of Commander Ruhullah , Haji Seyid Jan Khakrezwal's nephew, to secure Highway One from Kandahar to Kabul.

Ahmed Wali has thus already largely consolidated the PSCs in Kandahar under his influence, although the units retain their own commanders and individual unit names. He does not control all PSCs in Kandahar, however. Other powerbrokers, including Gul Agha Sherzai, the former governor of Kandahar and the current governor of Nangarhar, maintain private security forces in the province. For example, Gul Agha provides security for Haji Abdullah Khan (a wealthy banker and owner of the construction firm that built the houses in Aino Mena).[6] Further consolidation of private security forces in Kandahar may allow Ahmed Wali Karzai to bring his rivals' security forces under the control of a commander loyal and responsive to him.

The Kandahar Security Company

There have been reports of plans to consolidate PSCs in southern Afghanistan under the guidance of Ahmed Wali Karzai since March 2010, when Afghan Interior Minister Hanif Atmar was quoted as stating that Ahmed Wali Karzai was working with the MoI to bring as many as eighteen "unlicensed private security companies" in Kandahar Province under control.[7] These plans were approved by the MoI and forwarded to President Karzai's office for him to sign in mid-May.[8] The new security structure will bring local PSCs into a single organization, the Kandahar Security Company. According to the MoI, this force will start with only 500 employees, but there are suggestions that it may grow to 2,500 employees.[9]

Ruhullah has been identified as the probable commander of the new Kandahar Security Company.[10] Ruhullah is a Popalzai security commander who has built a powerful security network controlling much of Highway One between Kabul and Kandahar, and who is reportedly close to Ahmed Wali Karzai.[11] He is the nephew of Haji Seyid Jan Khakrezwal, a member of the provincial council and the commander of its private security force. Ruhullah consolidated control over the Kabul-Kandahar route after the assassination of rival commander Abdul Khaliq in the spring of 2009.[12]

The exact structure of the new Kandahar Security Company will likely be determined over the next several months, but Ruhullah's initial role as commander of the force suggests that his current network will have the leading role in the new structure and will likely subsume smaller PSCs. Abdul Manan Farahi, who heads the MoI's Counter-terrorism department and is charged with regulating PSCs, has stated that command of the Kandahar Security Company would rotate every six months.[13] But the feasibility of this arrangement seems questionable. And even if rotated, the formal command may well be subverted by the informal influence of individuals such as Ruhullah or Ahmed Wali Karzai.

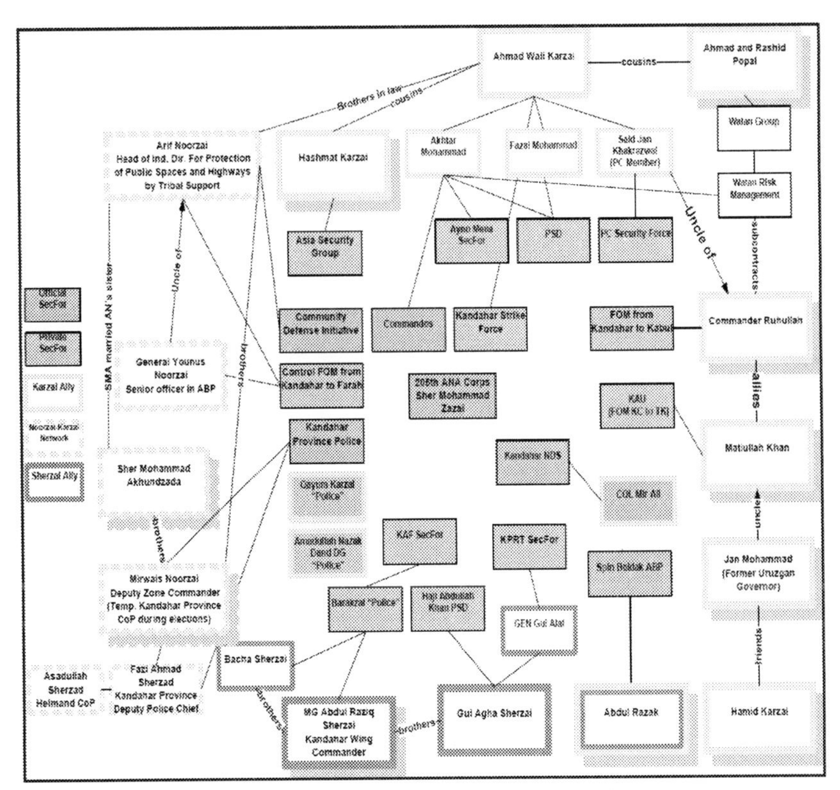

Credit: Kimberly Kagan and Frederick W. Kagan

Power-Brokers and Security Forces in Kandahar

The geographic confines of the Kandahar PSC consolidation are not clear. It is, however, rumored that a separate consolidation of PSCs providing highway security west of Kandahar is being considered. The highway security of that area would fall under the guidance of Arif Noorzai, the brother-in-law of Ahmed Wali Karzai and a close political ally of President Hamid Karzai. The Noorzai family, which is intermarried with the Farahi family in Farah province, has in the past used control over highways in southwest Afghanistan to facilitate smuggling. Any involvement by Arif Noorzai in PSC consolidation along Highway One should be a cause for further investigation.[14]

The Watan Ban

The same week that the plans to consolidate Kandahar's PSCs were forwarded to the President, two PSCs, Watan Risk Management and Compass Integrated Security Solutions, were banned from operating between Kabul and Kandahar.[15] The ban occurred after PSCs running security for logistics convoys opened fire on locals in Wardak Province in two separate incidents on May 8-9, 2010.[16]

The ban on Compass and Watan started on the morning of Monday, May 10, 2010. On that day logistics convoys leaving Kabul faced some of the largest ambushes of the year, with attacks conducted in Zanakhan, Rashidan, and Ghazni Districts of Ghazni Province.[17] Over the following week there were escalated attacks on logistics convoys moving from Kabul south to both Kandahar and to bases in Regional Command East, including significant clashes in the Moqor and Andar districts of Ghazni province .[18]

Watan, run by President Hamid Karzai's cousins Ahmed and Rateb Popal, has increased its influence over key transit routes in eastern and southern Afghanistan. Watan's main subcontractor between Kandahar and Kabul is the same commander Ruhullah who has been suggested as head of the Kandahar Security Company.[19] Ruhullah is reported to have sufficient influence over the Kabul to Kandahar route such that not only Watan, but almost all the logistics companies operating between Kabul and Kandahar are forced to subcontract with him to provide security. [20]

Because Ruhullah is considered the key player on the Kabul-Kandahar road, the increased attacks against ISAF convoys suggests that the ban against Watan operations also prevented Ruhullah, Watan's primary subcontractor, from conducting operations along Highway One.[21] Watan is unsurprisingly operating again as of May 18, after paying compensation to the families of those killed, but the connection between the Popal brothers and the Karzais poses interesting questions about why the administration did not intervene earlier to block the suspension of Watan's operations.[22]

Analysis

Watan has probably become a political liability for the Karzai family, which may well be trying to take steps publicly to seem to regulate the firm's behavior. It is noteworthy that Watan has come under intense media scrutiny in the last several months. The Karzais may feel that the firm will have difficulty withstanding intense investigation, and have subsequently decided to abandon it as a primary tool of their influence.[23] The MoI's ability to ban Watan operations for a week suggests that the Karzais may feel they can step away from the firm.

But if President Karzai and Ahmed Wali are indeed distancing themselves from Watan, they are not necessarily relinquishing private control over private security. Ruhullah has been suggested for command of the new PSC conglomerate in Kandahar. He is in effect not losing his job as a Watan security subcontractor, but rather getting promoted to command an expanded security force. His close relationship with Ahmed Wali Karzai persists, regardless of his relationship to Watan, and he will be under the influence of his Karzai family patrons.

The Karzai-affiliated network of private security forces is adaptable, and if need be can jettison corporate structures and find new ways to organize itself. In fact, a conglomerated Kandahar PSC under Ahmed Wali Karzai's influence might more effectively serve the interests of the Karzai inner-circle and family than did Watan. This new Kandahar Security Company would almost certainly extend Ahmed Wali's influence over the private security companies of his rivals in Kandahar by bringing them under Ruhullah's command.

Ahmed Wali Karzai has consistently aimed to bring local militias and PSCs under his influence. Both Watan Risk Management and Asia Security Group have been used to advance this objective by bringing a number of regional militias into the business network of the Karzai family.[24] But a conglomerated Kandahar PSC operating with the support of the MoI, which under the political influence of the Karzai administration, may ultimately allow the Karzai immediate family as much, if not more, control over armed groups than corporate structures like Watan or Asia Security Group – if indeed, Watan and Asia Security Group are among the eighteen companies consolidated by the MOI directive.

ISAF and the MoI have both publically stated an intention to address the problem of illegal private security contractors in Kandahar.[25] Ahmed Wali Karzai's leading role in the consolidation of PSCs into a single entity and his hand-selection of a commander allows him to present himself to ISAF as taking the lead on tackling the PSC problem in Kandahar – without relinquishing effective means of influence. Minister Atmar, meanwhile, may either be acquiescing freely or feel he has no other choice in Kandahar but to work with AWK.

The formation of a powerful conglomerate of PSCs under the political control of local powerbrokers like Ahmed Wali Karzai would undermine the long-term stability of southern Afghanistan and the strength of Afghanistan's legitimate security institutions. There is a very real risk that these institutions will be relied on by the Karzais and their allies as the guarantors of Kandahar's security. If the Kandahar Security Company were in fact to grow to 2,500 armed men as Ruhullah suggests (and this is certainly feasible) it would be more than twice the current size of the Afghan Uniformed Police in Kandahar, and would exceed the size of the expanded police force that ISAF and the MOI are planning to add to the city. The Karzais and their allies already use private militias as a substitute or for the Afghan National Security Forces (ANSF). Consolidating local militias into a body outside of the formal ANSF will continue to de-incentivize local powerbrokers from lending their support to the ANSF.

Recommendations

Ahmed Wali Karzai has reportedly been lobbying ISAF officials in favor of the Kandahar Security Company for some time.[26] It would behoove ISAF and the Afghan State for ISAF to play an active role in the discussions of the formation of any conglomerate private security force, in order to prevent local powerbrokers like Ahmed Wali Karzai from manipulating the process to their own ends. Without ISAF's intervention the MOI will have little choice but to accede to consolidating the new security force and allowing Ahmed Wali Karzai to have de facto influence over its actions inside the city, given the MoI's limited influence in Kandahar.

Rather than consolidating security companies, ISAF's aim should be to disband these armed units and replace them with ANSF. To achieve ANSF primacy, ISAF cannot simply incorporate these PSCs or their members into the formal security forces. It will be necessary to vet their members, retrain them, and disperse them throughout the country via the established national recruiting and assignment procedures. The army would better incorporate these militias than the police, because of its ability to assign forces nationally.

Shaping the formation of Kandahar's new private security architecture requires ISAF to engage in the process at an early stage and set the conditions for the creation of the new structure. ISAF should use its influence to remove the process from the control of local powerbrokers, such as Ahmed Wali Karzai or Ruhullah. ISAF should refuse to allow Ruhullah to command the new security force. A hands-off approach will allow these actors to present the new architecture to ISAF as a *fait accompli.*

ISAF ought to require that all PSC units be partnered with on the ground ISAF oversight teams co-located with the unit. These teams would function largely as do police mentors. They would provide much needed visibility on the actions and political links of these units. They could eventually give ISAF the ability to cut the links between these armed groups and their political patrons and then disband the units . ISAF partnership can also help to ensure legal compliance, professionalism, and political neutrality in the interval while the PSCs are vetted and disbanded.

ISAF will dramatically increase the risks to the success of its mission if it allows the formation of the new Kandahar Security Company. If that company is nevertheless formed, ISAF must ensure that the formal MoI chain-of-command selects a neutral new commander, has strong command and control relationships over the new structure, and oversees the initial and follow-on training for the unit. ISAF might also consider the formation of a board of directors at the MoI to oversee the new body, composed of individuals without entrenched interests in southern Afghanistan, mentored by ISAF, and sufficiently sheltered from political pressure. The board would initially need active and interventionist ISAF support on the ground in Kabul and Kandahar if it would hope to exert control over the new security structure. Alternatively, ISAF might consider putting the new security structure under the control of the ANA.

End Notes

[1] "DoD News Briefing with Maj, Gen. Carter," Department of Defense News Transcripts, http://www.defense.gov/transcripts/transcript.aspx?transcriptid=4436, May 26, 2010.

[2] Jake Sherman and Victoria DiDomenico, "The Public Cost of Private Security in Afghanistan," Center on International Cooperation, New York University, September, 2009, pg 5.

[3] Aram Roston, "How the US Funds the Taliban," *The Nation*, November 11, 2009.

[4] Dexter Filkins, Mark Mazzetti, and James Risen, "Brother of CIA Leader Said to Be Paid by C.I.A.," *New York Times*, October 27, 2009.

[5] "Kandahar City Municipality & Dand District, District Narrative Analysis," Stability Operations Center Kabul, March 30, 2010. Accessed through google: <http://webcache.googleusercontent.com/search?q=cache:txKkli8M4I8J:https://strykernet2.army.mil/LessonsLearned/Lessons_Learned_AAR_OIL/Intelligence_(INTEL)/COIN_Kandahar_City_district_narrative_UNCLASS%252030%2520Mar%25202010.pdf+%22Kandahar+City+Municipality%22+%26+Dand+district&cd=1&hl=en&ct=clnk&gl=us>

[6] "Kandahar City Municipality & Dand District, District Narrative Analysis," Stability Operations Center Kabul,
March 30, 2010. Accessed through google:

<http://webcache.googleusercontent.com/search?q=cache:txKkli8M4I8J:https://strykernet2.army.mil/LessonsLearned/Lessons_Learned_AAR_OIL/Intelligence_(INTEL)/COIN_Kandahar_City_district_narrative_UNCLASS%252030%2520Mar%25202010.pdf+%22Kandahar+City+Municipality%22+%26+Dand+district&cd=1&hl=en&ct=clnk&gl=us>

[7] Dexter Filkins, "Despite Doubt, Karzai Brother Retains Power," *The New York Times*, March 30, 2010.

[8] Dion Nissenbaum, "Afghan Security Deal Could Boost President Karzai's Half-Brother," McClatchy, May 20, 2010.

[9] Dion Nissenbaum, "Afghan Security Deal Could Boost President Karzai's Half-Brother," McClatchy, May 20, 2010; Dexter Filkins, "Despite Doubt, Karzai Brother Retains Power," *The New York Times*, March 30, 2010; Matthew Green, "Afghan Warlords Feed on US Contracts, Say Critics," Financial Times, May 11, 2010

[10] Dion Nissenbaum, "Afghan Security Deal Could Boost President Karzai's Half-Brother," McClatchy, May 20, 2010.

[11] Carl Forsberg, "Politics and Power in Kandahar," Institute for the Study of War, April 2010, 38.

[12] Aram Roston, "How the US Funds the Taliban," *The Nation*, November 11, 2009.

[13] Dion Nissenbaum, "Afghan Security Deal Could Boost President Karzai's Half-Brother," McClatchy, May 20, 2010.

[14] Carl Forsberg, "Politics and Power in Kandahar," Institute for the Study of War, April 2010, 34-5.

[15] Hakim Basharat, "2 Security Companies Banned from Kabul-Kandahar Highway," Pajhwok Afghan News, May 9, 2010; Agence France Presse, "Afghansitan Bars Security Firms after Civilian Deaths," May 9, 2010.

[16] Hakim Basharat, "2 Security Companies Banned from Kabul-Kandahar Highway," Pajhwok Afghan News, May 9, 2010; Agence France Presse, "Afghansitan Bars Security Firms after Civilian Deaths," May 9, 2010.

[17] Afghan Islamic Press News Agency, "Three Taliban Killed in Afghan East – Officials," BBC Monitoring South Asia – Political, May 10, 2010; Mirwais Himmat, "Two Taliban Killed in Ghazni," Pajhwok Afghan News, May 11, 2010.

[18] Afghan Islamic Press News Agency, "NATO Logistic Convoy Comes Under Taleban Attack in Afghan Southwest," BBC Monitoring South Asia – Political," May 14, 2010; Rahim Faiez, "At Least 30 Militants Dead in Afghan, NATO Raids," Associated Press, May 15, 2010. Rahim Faiez, "At Least 30 Militants Dead in Afghan, NATO Raids," Associated Press, May 15, 2010; Mirwais Himmat and Azizi, "Four Killed in Separate Incidents," Pajhwok Afghan News, May 16, 2010.

[19] Carl Forsberg, "Politics and Power in Kandahar," Institute for the Study of War, April 2010, 38.

[20] Aram Roston, "How the US Funds the Taliban," The Nation, November 11, 2009.

[21] Aram Roston, "How the US Funds the Taliban," The Nation, November 11, 2009.

[22] One story is that ban was the result of a long-time antagonism between the governor of Wardak Province, Muhammad Fidai, and Watan Security group. Governor Fidai is reported to have, for some time, been attempting to make power plays against Watan, and replace Ruhullah's control over route security with interests connected to himself, and civilian casualties may have given him the necessary cover to do so. But the story seems more complex than that, because the Karzai administration presumably has enough influence over the MoI to have blocked the move if it had desired to do so.

[23] See for example, Aram Roston, "How the US Funds the Taliban," *The Nation,* November 30, 2009; CBC News, "Taliban Protection Pay-offs Denied by Contractor," April 27, 2010; and Matthew Green, "Afghan Warlords Feed on US Contracts, Say Critics," Financial Times, May 11, 2010.

[24] Carl Forsberg, "Politics and Power in Kandahar," Institute for the Study of War, April 2010, 27-31.

[25] Caroline Wyatt, "NATO Troops Prepare Kandahar Push," BBC News, May 14, 2010.

[26] Dion Nissenbaum, "Afghan Security Deal Could Boost President Karzai's Half-Brother," McClatchy, May 20, 2010.

In: Corruption, Contractors, and Warlords... ISBN: 978-1-61761-598-6
Editor: Jacob E. Jankowski © 2011 Nova Science Publishers, Inc.

Chapter 8

WRITTEN STATEMENT OF DR. T. X. HAMMES, SENIOR RESEARCH FELLOW, BEFORE THE SUBCOMMITTEE ON NATIONAL SECURITY AND FOREIGN AFFAIRS, HEARING ON "INVESTIGATION OF PROTECTION PAYMENTS FOR SAFE PASSAGE ALONG THE AFGHAN SUPPLY CHAIN"

PRIVATE CONTRACTORS IN WARZONES: THE GOOD, THE BAD AND THE QUESTION

In Iraq and Afghanistan, the use of contractors has reached a level unprecedented in U.S. military operations. In September 2009, contractors represented 47% of DOD's workforce in Iraq and 62% in Afghanistan.[1] The presence of contractors on the battlefield is obviously not a new phenomenon but decisions made over the last few decades have dramatically increased DoD's reliance on them to execute its basic missions. First, force structure reductions ranging from the post-Vietnam decisions to move the majority of Army logistics support elements to the Army Reserve and Guard[2] to the post-Cold War reduction in force decisions that reduced the Army from 18 to 10 divisions greatly reduced the services' ability to support long-term operations. Next came a series of decisions that led to the wider employment of contractors in the Balkans during the 1990s. Finally, the decision to invade

Iraq with a minimum of force left the U.S. with too few troops to deal with the disorder that resulted from the removal of the regime. Thus it is understandable that given the immediate, unanticipated need for large numbers of logistics and security personnel, the shortage of such troops on active duty and the precedent for using contractors in the Balkans, the Pentagon turned to contractors to fill the immediate needs. However, the subsequent failure to conduct a careful analysis of the wisdom of using contractors is less understandable. For the purposes of this chapter, the services provided by private contractors will include both armed and unarmed services. While the U.S. government has conducted and continues to conduct numerous investigations into fraud, waste and corruption in the contracting process, it has not yet systematically explored the essential question -- "Is it strategically a good idea to use contractors in counterinsurgency operations or even military operations in general?"

This article will make an effort to explore that question. It will examine the positive aspects of wartime contracting, the negative aspects and finally the strategic question of whether contractors should or should not be employed. In short, it will explore the good, the bad and the real question.

THE GOOD

One of the primary advantages of private contractors is their ability to quickly mobilize and deploy large numbers of personnel. This is particularly important when the base plan fails to anticipate problems. Since the Pentagon had not planned to keep large numbers of troops in Afghanistan or Iraq for any period of time, it had not planned for the required logistics support. The Pentagon also failed to anticipate the requirement for large numbers of security personnel to protect all U.S. activities, even political and reconstruction activities, once the Afghan and Iraqi governments were toppled.

By tapping into data bases, running job fairs in the United States and contracting for labor from third world companies, contractors were able to quickly recruit, process and ship personnel to run base camps, man convoys, and perform the hundreds of housekeeping chores required to maintain both combat forces and civil administrators spread across Iraq and Afghanistan. More challenging was finding qualified personnel to provide security for the rapidly growing U.S. presence in both nations. The private companies managed to find people, hire them and move them into country – all without the political problems inherent in mobilizing additional U.S. military forces to execute the same tasks. The combination of speed and a low political profile made contractors an attractive choice to provide the resources the administration had failed to plan for. Both inside and outside Iraq and Afghanistan, contractors replaced the thousands of soldiers normally required to move, stage, marshal and transport personnel and supplies into the combat zone.[3]

Continuity is a second major advantage of contractors. While the U.S. military has a policy that insures the vast majority of personnel rotate every 6-12 months, contractors are often willing to stay for longer periods. For key billets, companies can offer significant bonuses to personnel who stay. The companies know they will reap commensurate savings due to the personnel continuity and the personnel see an opportunity for significantly increased pay.

However, the most highly prized attribute of private contractors is that they replace troops. As late as April 2008, the Department of Defense stated it had 163,900 contractors supporting 160,000 troops in Iraq.[4] Without the presence of contractors, the United States would have had to provide literally twice as many troops at the height of operations. The U.S. Armed Forces struggled to maintain 160,000 troops in Iraq, it is very doubtful they could have supported the 320,000 needed if contractors were not employed. While the vast majority of the contractor personnel were involved in non-combatant logistics tasks, the Department of Defense estimated there were over 20,000 armed contractors in Iraq during 2007. Other organizations' estimates are much higher.[5] Even using the Pentagon's lower estimate, contractors provided three times more armed troops than the British and replaced more than a division of U.S. troops. It should also be noted that in Iraq and Afghanistan many of the unarmed, logistic support personnel functioned in an essentially combat role. The drivers were subject to both IED and direct fire attacks despite the fact they were not trained or equipped for those situations. The contractors not only provided relief in terms of personnel tempo but also absorbed over 25% of the killed in action in Iraq. Contractors reported almost 1800 dead and 40,000 wounded by the end of 2009.[6] For all practical purposes, these casualties were "off the books" in that they had no real impact on the political discussions about the war. As Peter Singer noted,

> "there was no outcry whenever contractors were called up and deployed, or even killed. If the gradual death toll among American troops threatened to slowly wear down public support, contractor casualties were not counted in official death tolls and had no impact on these ratings. … These figures mean

that the private military industry has suffered more losses in Iraq than the rest of the coalition of allied nations combined. The losses are also far more than any single U.S. Army division has experienced." [7]

Of course, it is difficult if not impossible to determine how many additional casualties were suffered by Third World Nation contractors in either Iraq or Afghanistan.

Replacing these contractors, both armed and unarmed, would have required additional major mobilizations of reserves or a dramatic increase in end strength for the Army and Marine Corps. In effect, the rapid mobilization of civilian contractors allowed the United States to engage in a protracted conflict in Iraq without the necessity of convincing the U.S. public of the need for mobilization or major increases in the active Armed Forces to do so. Opponents of contractors point out that this makes it easier for U.S. political leaders to commit forces to protracted conflicts precisely because it reduces uniformed casualties.[8] Whether or not the tendency of contractors to reduce the political cost of operations is a good thing or not depends upon your view of the particular conflict.

Another advantage frequently cited by proponents of the use of contractors is that of cost. According to their calculations, contractors are much cheaper to use than government employees. In fact, the actual costs remain a point of contention. The Congressional Research Service stated it was "The relative cost advantage of the contractors can vary, and may diminish or disappear altogether, depending on the circumstances and contract."[9] Determining actual costs is extremely difficult due to the large number of variables involved – some of them currently unknowable. For instance, with over 40,000 contractors wounded to date, we are unable to estimate potential long-term care costs to the USG. While contractors may claim their insurance covers those costs, in fact, the government paid for that insurance through the contract and, if the coverage proves insufficient, the government may well end up paying for the continued care through various government medical programs. In short, costs associated with employing contractors in a combat environment are essentially unknowable.

Another useful aspect of contracting is hiring locals to provide services. Creating jobs and stimulating the economy are key aspects of population-centric counterinsurgency. In the Balkans and Afghanistan, NATO and ISAF have hired large numbers of local personnel to conduct both armed and unarmed tasks. However, even increased employment has potential downsides that will be discussed in the next section.

A final, critical advantage is that contractors may be able to do jobs U.S. forces simply can't. In Afghanistan, we lack the forces to provide security for our primary supply lines to Pakistan because they run through areas either controlled or heavily contested by the Taliban or other organizations that charge for use of the road. However, if history is any guide, even a heavy presence of U.S. troops would not guarantee the delivery of supplies. Fortunately, Afghan contractors display the mix of force, personal connections and negotiation skills to maintain our supply lines.

THE BAD

When serving within the combat zone, particularly during a counterinsurgency, contractors create a number of significant problems from the tactical to the strategic level. Three primary characteristics of contractors, particularly armed contractors, create problems for the government. First, the government does not control the quality of the personnel the contractor hires. Second, unless it provides a government officer or NCO for each convoy, personal security detail or facilities protection unit, it does not control their daily interactions with the local population. Finally, the population holds the government responsible for everything the contractors do or fail to do. Since insurgency is essentially a competition for legitimacy between the government and insurgents, this factor elevates the issue of quality and tactical control to the strategic level.

Quality control is a well publicized issue. The repeated reports of substandard construction, fraud and theft highlight the problems associated with unarmed contractors. As noted above, these incidents are being investigated. In addition, the USG is working hard to refine contracting and oversight procedures to reduce these types of problems. Unfortunately, the problem is just as prevalent with armed contractors. While high-end personal security details generally are well trained, less visible armed contractors display less quality. When suicide bombers began striking Iraqi Armed Forces recruiting stations, the contractor responsible for recruiting the Iraqi forces subcontracted for a security force. The contractor was promised former Gurkhas. What showed up in Iraq a couple of weeks later were untrained, under-equipped Nepalese villagers.[10] Not only did these contractors provide inadequate security, the U.S. government passed the authority to use deadly force in the name of the United States to these untrained foreign nationals.

Since the government neither recruits nor trains individual armed contractors, it essentially has to trust the contractor to provide quality personnel. In this case, the subcontractor took shortcuts despite the obvious risk to the personnel manning the recruiting stations. Even if we hire enough contracting officers to effectively supervise the contracts, how exactly does a contracting officer determine the military qualifications of an individual much less a group such as a Personal or Site Security Detail? The U.S. military dedicates large facilities, major exercises, expensive simulations and combat experienced staffs to determine if U.S. units are properly trained. Contractors don't. We need to acknowledge that contracting officers have no truly effective control over the quality of the personnel the contractors hire. In fact, we have to accept that we will be unable to determine their actual effectiveness until they begin to operate in theater. And then, only if a member of the U.S. government is in position to observe the contractors as they operate.

Compounding the problems created by lack of quality control, the government does not control the contractor's daily contact with the population. Despite continued efforts to increase government oversight of contractor operations, nothing short of having qualified U.S. government personnel accompanying and in command of the contractors will provide control. With support contractors this means we may get poorly wired buildings or malfunctioning computer systems. However, with armed contractors we have the bullying, intimidation and even killing of local civilians such as the September 2007 Blackwater shootings in Nisour Square.

The lack of quality and tactical control greatly increase the impact of the third major problem – the United States is held responsible for everything the contractors do or fail to do. Despite the fact the United States has no effective quality or operational control over the contractors, the local population rightly holds it responsible for all contractor failures. Numerous personal conversations with Iraqis revealed a deep disgust with the actions of armed contractors. They noted we gave them authority to use deadly weapons in our name. While Iraqis were not confident American forces would be punished for killing Iraqis, they believed it was at least a possibility. However, the Iraqis were convinced that contractors were simply above any law.

These perceptions serious undercut the legitimacy of the government. A key measure of the legitimacy of a government is a monopoly on the use of force within its boundaries. The very act of hiring armed contractors dilutes that monopoly. Legitimate governments are also responsible for the actions of their agents – particularly those actions taken against their own populations.

Yet, despite efforts to increase the accountability of contractors, the widespread perception is that armed contractors who commit crimes against host nation people are outside the law of both the host country and the United States. While we have laws criminalizing certain activities, the cost and difficulty of trying a contractor for crimes that occurred overseas in a conflict zone has so far deterred U.S. prosecutors. In over seven years of activity in Iraq, no contractor has been convicted of a crime against Iraqi citizens. Either contractors are a remarkably law abiding group or the system does not work. The fact that an insurgency is essentially a competition for legitimacy in the eyes of the people elevates the presence of armed contractors to a strategic issue.

Exacerbating the legitimacy issue, contractors of all kinds are a serious irritant to the host nation population. Armed contractors irritate because they are an unaccountable group that can and does impose its will upon the population in many daily encounters – driving too fast, forcing locals off the road, using the wrong side of the road. Even unarmed contractors irritate the population when they take relatively well paying jobs that local people desperately need.

In addition to undercutting its legitimacy, the use of contractors may actually undercut local government power. In Afghanistan, security and reconstruction contracts have resulted in significant shifts in relative power between competing Afghan qawms as well as allegations of corruption. Dexter Filkins, writing in the *NY Times* notes the power structure in Orugzan Province, Afghanistan has changed completely due to the U.S. government selecting Mr. Matiullah Khan to provide security for convoys from Kandahar to Tirin Kot.

> "With his NATO millions, and the American backing, Mr. Matiullah has grown into the strongest political and economic force in the region. He estimates that his salaries support 15,000 people in this impoverished province. … This has irritated some local leaders, who say that the line between Mr. Matiullah's business interest and the government has disappeared. …. Both General Carter and Hanif Atmar, the Afghan interior minister, said they hoped to disband Mr. Matiullah's militia soon — or at least to bring it under formal government control. … General Carter said that while he had no direct proof in Mr. Matiullah's case, he harbored more general worries that the legions of unregulated Afghan security companies had a financial interest in prolonging chaos."[11]

Thus, an unacknowledged but very serious strategic impact of using contractors is to directly undercut both the legitimacy and the authority of the host nation government.

Contracting also has a direct and measureable impact on the local economy. When the U.S. government passes its authority to a prime contractor, that contractor then controls a major source of new wealth and power in the community. However, the contractor is motivated by two factors – maximizing profit and making his operation run smoothly. This means that even if he devotes resources to understanding the impact of his operations on society, his decisions on how to allocate those resources will be different than those of someone trying to govern the area. For instance, various contractors' policies of hiring South Asians rather than Iraqis caused anger among Iraqis during the critical early phases of the insurgency. Desperate for jobs, the Iraqis saw Third Country Nationals getting jobs Iraqis were both qualified for and eager to do.[12] While there were clear business reasons and some security reasons for doing so, the decision was a slap in the face of Iraqis at a time of record unemployment within the country.

In contrast, the U.S. government in the form of a Provincial Reconstruction Team or a U.S. commander writes contracts specifically to influence the political and security situation in the area.

A related problem is the perception of the local population concerning how these contracts are managed. In Afghanistan, many Afghans are convinced that some contracts expend up to 80% of the funds on management. Agency Coordinating Body for Afghan Relief states 40% of the aid goes straight to corporate profit and salaries. Profit margins run as high as 50% and full time ex-patriot consultants cost between $250,000 and $350,000 per year.[13] Many of the contracts run through multiple subcontracting companies before the aid reaches the Afghan people and each subcontractor naturally takes a percentage for administrative overhead.[14] These confirmed cases of misuse of development funds further reduce the weak legitimacy of the Afghan government as well as ISAF's efforts.

There are also a number of indirect consequences of employing armed contractors. First, it opens the door for local organizations to build militias under the cover of being a security company. It is difficult to object to other elements of a society hiring security when the government is doing so. This is particularly true when the government is hiring both locals and foreign nationals to provide security. If the government needs private contractors to feel safe, the citizens, local businesses or even local political organizations can certainly argue that they do too. This fact has created significant problems for ISAF in Afghanistan.

> "Because PSCs are under the control of powerful individuals, rather than the Afghan National Security Forces, they compete with state security forces and interfere with a government monopoly on the use of force. There is growing pressure from ISAF and within the Afghan government to reform and regulate these companies. Major General Nick Carter, the commander of Regional Command-South (RC-S), recently briefed that ISAF was developing a strategy to regulate PSCs as part of the Kandahar Operations unfolding in summer 2010."[15]

In addition, Private Security Companies can compete directly with host nation attempts to recruit and retain military and police personnel In January 2010, Major General Michael Ward stated that Afghanistan's government was considering capping the pay of private security firms because Afghan police were deserting in large numbers for the better pay and working conditions associated with private companies.[16] This has created significant problems for ISAF. Major General Nick Carter, UK Army and Commander, ISAF Regional Command-South told reporters

> "(P)rivate security companies and militias are a serious problem … this is, of course, something that is of our own creation to a degree … where we contracted out everything to the civilian market, has created these private security companies. And of course they are paid a great deal more than our Afghan security forces, which in itself is counterproductive because, of course, the temptation for a soldier in the ANP is to go across to a private security company because he might earn double in pay."[17]

Contract hiring also competes directly with the host nation civil government. In both Iraq and Afghanistan, educated professionals took jobs as drivers or clerks with contractors and NGOs simply because the jobs paid more than they could earn working for their own governments. In effect, ISAF and NGO hiring has created an internal "brain drain." This is of particular concern in Afghanistan where human capital is a major limitation on the ability of the government to function.

Contractors, both armed and unarmed, also represent a serious military vulnerability. In the uprising in the spring of 2004 when both Sunni and Shia factions conducted major operations against Coalition forces, the insurgents effectively cut Allied supply lines from Kuwait. U.S. forces faced significant logistics challenges as a result. Despite the crisis, U.S. officials could not morally order contract logistics providers to "fight through." The contractors lacked the training, equipment and legal status to do so. Had the supply line been run by military forces, it would have been both moral and possible to order them to fight through. Despite this demonstrated operational vulnerability, the fact that unarmed contractors are specifically not obligated to fight through has not been emphasized as a significant risk in employing contractors rather than military logistics organizations.

The substitution of contractors for soldiers and Marines creates yet another vulnerability – lack of an emergency reserve. In the past, support troops have been repeatedly employed in critical situations to provide reinforcements for overwhelmed combat troops. Contractors are simply unable to fulfill this emergency role. This limitation, as well as the contractor's inability to fight through, are even more significant in conventional conflicts than in irregular war.

Contracting also takes key element of the counterinsurgency effort out of the hands of the commander. In the spring of 2010, ISAF determined that DynCorp had failed in its contract to train and mentor the Afghan police. ISAF then put the contract out for competition. Commander ISAF stated that the police are one the most critical elements of his campaign plan so the contracting process was accelerated. Not surprisingly, DynCorp did not win the new contract. Since time is critical in Afghanistan, plans were made to rapidly transition the contract to a new provider to insure the Afghan police could play their part in the COIN campaign. However, DynCorp protested the contract award and won in court. Thus they retain the training contract and will retain it while all legal processes are exhausted. In short, the commander lost control of one of the critical elements of his counterinsurgency campaign at a critical time -- and there is nothing he can do about it. Despite DynCorp's documented failure, it remains in charge of police training and mentoring with the full knowledge that as soon as possible ISAF will get rid of them.

Contracts also fragment the chain of command. While all military units in a theater are under the command of the senior military officer in the theater, contractors are not. While both contractors and the government have worked hard to resolve coordination issues, the fact remains the contractors are not under military command.

A final negative impact of contracting is the requirement to provide security for unarmed contractors. Military logistics units can provide their own security in low threat environments but unarmed contractors cannot. The government must either assign military forces or hire additional armed contractors to provide that security.

The Question

Clearly contractors have an important and continuing role in U.S. operations – both domestic and overseas. In fact, there are currently numerous functions the United States Government is incapable of performing without contractor support. This is not a new phenomenon. DoD – particularly the Air Force and Navy – have long relied on contractors to fill niche requirements such as maintaining and, sometimes, even operating the newest high technology equipment. However, in Iraq and Afghanistan, the USG is using contractors to execute functions in the field that bring them in daily contact with local populations in combat zones.

Despite conducting almost nine years of combat operations supported by contractors, the United States still has not conducted an in-depth study of the strategic impact the use of contractors has in counterinsurgency. I don't mean contracts and contractors are not being studied. Congress formed The Commission on Wartime Contracting specifically "to assess a number of factors related to wartime contracting, including the extent of waste, fraud, abuse, and mismanagement of wartime contracts."[18] While looking to improve the efficiency of wartime contracting, the Commission is not looking into the strategic impact the use of contractors has in COIN operations. In the executive summary of its June 2009 Interim Report, the Commission does not consider the strategic logic behind using contractors but instead, as tasked, focuses on improving efficiency.[19]

For their parts, the Departments of Defense and State are conducting studies to determine how to reduce fraud and increase the efficiency of contractors. The Joint Staff is running a major study to determine the level of dependency on contractor support in contingency operations. Various Justice Department investigations are going over past contracts for everything from fraud to abuse of prisoners to inappropriate use of deadly force. Yet none of these studies are looking at the fundamental questions concerning the strategic impact of contractors in combat.

Despite our failure to evaluate them, contractors clearly have a number of direct, strategic-level impacts on counterinsurgency operations. The most important are the reduction of political capital necessary to commit U.S. forces to war; the impacts on the legitimacy of a counterinsurgency effort; and the perceived morality of that effort.

Rather than automatically defaulting to hiring contractors as a relatively quick, easy and politically benign solution to an immediate problem, the United States needs to examine these strategic level questions.

First, what is the impact of contractors on the initial decision to go to war as well as the will to sustain the conflict? Both proponents and opponents admit the U.S. would have required much greater mobilization to support a force of 320,000 in Iraq (the combined troop and contractor count) or a force of over 210,000 in Afghanistan. The use of contractors allowed us to conduct both wars with much less domestic political discourse. But is this a good idea? Should we seek methods that make it easier to take the nation to war? That does not seem to be the intent of the Constitution nor does it seem like a good idea when entering protracted conflicts. Insurgents understand that political will is the critical vulnerability of the United States in irregular warfare. They have discussed this factor openly in their online strategic forums for almost a decade.[20] Insuring the American public understands the difficulty of the impending conflict and is firmly behind the effort should be an essential element in committing forces to such a conflict. Thus while the use of contractors lessons the extent of mobilization needed, it may well hurt the effort in the long term.

Second, as discussed earlier in this paper contractors undermine the legitimacy of both U.S. and host nation efforts in a counterinsurgency in a variety of ways. *FM 3-24 Counterinsurgency* states that the conflict is a competition for legitimacy between the counterinsurgent and the insurgent.[21] By choosing to use contractors, we directly undercut a central theme of our own counterinsurgency doctrine. Under certain conditions, we may choose to use contractors in spite of the impact on legitimacy but we should not do so in ignorance of that impact. Any decision to use contractors in a combat zone should be carefully considered for its impact on the strategy we have chosen and the campaign plan we are using to execute that strategy.

A third area which needs consideration at the strategic level is the morality of using contractors. What are the moral implications of authorizing contractors, qualified or not, to use deadly force in the name of the United States? What about hiring poor third world citizens to sustain casualties in support of U.S. policy? What is the U.S. responsibility for wounded and killed contractors – particularly third world contractors? While these sound like theoretical questions, they are in fact practical ones. Maintaining domestic popular support for conflict requires that it U.S. actions be both legitimate and moral.

These questions are essentially derived from the real question "Is it strategically a good idea to use contractors in combat zones?" While it is too late to debate this question for our current conflicts, it is essential we make this a central part of our post-Afghanistan force structure discussions. The size and type of force we build for the future depends on the answer.

The views expressed in this statement are those of the author and do not reflect the official policy or position of the National Defense University, the Defense Department or the U.S. government.

End Notes

[1] Moshe Schwartz, "Department of Defense Contractors in Iraq and Afghanistan: Background and Analysis," Congressional Research Service, 14 Dec 2009.

[2] Peter W. Singer, "The Dark Truth About Blackwater," *Salon*, October 2, 2007, http://www.salon. com/news/feature/2007/10/02/blackwater/print.html, accessed 22 Dec 2009.

[3] Dan Baum, "Nation Builders for Hire," *New York Times*, http://www.information clearinghouse.info/ article3905.htm, accessed 29 Dec 2009.

[4] "Wising up, moving out," *Jane's Defense Weekly*, 1 July 2009, p. 29.

[5] Fainaru, Steve, "Private War: Convoy to Darkness," *Washington Post*, Jul 29, 2007, p. 1.

[6] http://icasualties.org and http://www.propublica.org/series/disposable-army, accessed 29 Dec 2009.

[7] Peter W. Singer, "The Dark Truth About Blackwater," *Salon*, October 2, 2007, http://www.salon.com/ news/feature/2007/10/02/blackwater/print.html.

[8] David Isenberg, "Private Military Contractors and U.S. Grand Strategy," International Peace Research Institute, Oslo, Norway, January 2009, p. 5.

[9] Jennifer K. Elsea, Moshe Schwartz and Kennon H. Nakamura, "Private Security Contractors in Iraq: Background , Legal Status, and Other Issues, *Congressional Research Service*, Updated Aug 25, 2008, p. 49.

[10] Author's personal experience will serving on Coalition Military Assistance Training Team in Iraq during early 2004.

[11] Dexter Filkins, "With US Aid, Warlord Builds Afghan Empire," *NY Times*, 6 Jun 2010, http://www.nytimes. com/2010/06/06/world/asia/06warlords.html, accessed 7 June 2010.

[12] Nicholas Pelham, "Contractors in Iraq Accused of Importing Labor and Exporting Profit," *Financial Times*, 14 Oct 2003. http://www.commondreams.org/headlines03/1014-01.htm, accessed 7 Jun 2010

[13] Matt Waldman, "Falling Short: Aid Effectiveness in Afghanistan," ACBAR, http://www.acbar.org/ ACBAR%20Publications/ACBAR%20Aid%20Effectiveness%20(25%20Mar %2008).pdf, accessed 4 Jan 2010.

[14] Roya Wolverson, "Not So Helpful," *Newsweek, 24 Nov 2007*, http://www.newsweek.com/id/72068, accessed 4 Jan 2010.

[15] Carl Forsberg and Kimberly Kagan, "Consolidating Private Security Companies in South Afghanistan," *Institute for the Study of War*, 28 May 2010, http://www.understandingwar .org/files/BackgrounderPSC.pdf , accessed 4 Jun 2010.

[16] "Afghan-Cda Security Firms," The Canadian Press-Broadcase wire, 25 January 2010, 06:42. Document BNW0000020100126e61p00011.

[17] Major General Nick Carter's Defense Department Briefing via teleconference from Afghanistan, 26 May 2010.

[18] www.wartimecontracting.gov accessed 24 Jul 2009.

[19] Commission on Wartime Contracting in Iraq and Afghanistan, "At What Cost? Contingency Contracting in Iraq and Afghanistan, June 2009, http://www.wartimecontracting.gov /docs/CWC_ Interim_Report_At_What_ Cost_06-10-09.pdf, accessed 13 June 2010.

[20] MEMRI, "Bin Laden Lieutenant Admits to September 11 and Explains Al-Qa'ida's Combat Doctrine," 20 Feb 2002, http://www.memri.org/report/en/0/0/0/0/0/0/607.htm, accessed 13 Jun 2010

[21] *FM 3-24/MCWP3.33-5 Counterinsurgency*, Headquarters, Department of the Army, Dec 2006, p. 1-1.

In: Corruption, Contractors, and Warlords... ISBN: 978-1-61761-598-6
Editor: Jacob E. Jankowski © 2011 Nova Science Publishers, Inc.

Chapter 9

TESTIMONY OF S. FREDERICK STARR, CHAIRMAN, CENTRAL ASIA-CAUCASUS INSTITUTE, SCHOOL OF ADVANCED INTERNATIONAL AFFAIRS, JOHNS HOPKINS UNIVERSITY, BEFORE THE SUBCOMMITTEE ON NATIONAL SECURITY AND FOREIGN AFFAIRS, HEARING ON "INVESTIGATION OF PROTECTION PAYMENTS FOR SAFE PASSAGE ALONG THE AFGHAN SUPPLY CHAIN"

21 June 2010

The Subcommittee has expressed concern over the practice of making payments to local warlords and even Taliban forces to secure the transit of goods through the territories they control. Opponents of the practice see it as corrupt in principle and an unnecessary acknowledgment of the Taliban's authority in areas of primary concern to the US/NATO campaign. Defenders see it instead as a necessary means of securing a greater end, namely, the advancement of the current strategy of gaining control over territories, holding them, and then promoting forms of development that the local population will welcome. In this light, the practice becomes as tactical means of making the Taliban complicit in its own destruction as an effective force.

I am not going to adjudicate between these two alternatives as they have been presented here and as they are generally discussed today. Each can and does claim the high ground of principle and strategic prudence. I would like instead to focus your attention on the roads themselves, and on their absolute significance to the task in which we are engaged in Afghanistan. We tend to view them as simply the channels by which we deliver military equipment and supplies to our local forces. This is how we have conceived the Northern Distribution Network (NDN), the magnificent set of road and railroad routes that are moving more goods into Afghanistan today than has ever occurred in that country's history. In this case, as with the interior roads that we are securing through payments to the Taliban, the goods are essential to NATO's military mission.

But roads in Afghanistan and between Afghanistan and its neighbors potentially fulfill even more important functions, ones that pertain to the lives of everyone living in the area and to every government involved.

These functions include:

1. Links between farmers in remote areas and secondary markets.
2. Links between secondary and primary markets.
3. Links between primary markets and markets abroad.
4. Links along a continent-wide system of road transport that extends from Europe and the Middle East to India and Southeast Asia.
5. Thanks to the above four factors, roads are the most effective engines for profit to local farmers and processors, and the most efficient incubators of new industries and employment for Afghanistan as a whole, whether in the transport, processing, extractive or service sectors.

President Obama, like President Bush before him, has rightly stressed what is called the "economic" dimension of US strategy in Afghanistan. Without economic progress, no military gains will be solid or sustainable. Indeed, one can go as far as to say that unless the local populace is convinced that the US presence will improve their lives, even short-term military gains will be all but impossible. Stated differently, the US' stated goals of destroying al Queda and crippling the Taliban do not themselves engage local people. Only positive goals will bring them around, and this means the realistic hope of economic improvements for themselves and their families. Because of the five points listed above, the reopening of roads and transport routes within and across Afghanistan is not only the best but the *only* way of making battlefield gains permanent. Indeed, they are the key to success in Afghanistan.

Dr. Andrew C. Kuchins of CSIS and I, working with a team of experts, have prepared a brief paper on the central importance of roads and transport to our success in Afghanistan. Copies are available here today. David Ignatius provided a solid overview of the argument in last Sunday's *Washington Post*.

We argue that roads and other forms of transport, including railroads, pipelines and hydroelectric lines, are together a money machine that can fundamentally transform both Afghanistan and its neighbors. We point out that the reopening of these great transport routes within and through Afghanistan is advancing quickly with many patrons besides the United States. Among those investing billions to reopen continental trade are the Asian Development Bank, World Bank, and the governments of India, China, Pakistan, the EU, Russia, Iran, and all the countries of Central Asia and the Caucasus. No change taking place in the world today will do more to improve the lives of millions than this.

In the emergence of these grand networks, Afghanistan stands as a kind of bottleneck or cork. The old Soviet border effectively sliced through the "Silk Roads" that ran across Afghanistan, connecting India and Europe. Even after the collapse of the USSR, Afghanistan remained the great blockage in the system due to Taliban rule there.

The greatest result of Operation Enduring Freedom was not foreseen, intended, or even recognized at the time: by destroying Taliban rule the US opened the possibility of reviving the great transport routes across Afghanistan that had enabled that country to prosper for 2,000 years. If this happens, ordinary Afghans will be the beneficiaries, for they will be able to sell their agricultural produce at higher-priced markets, get their minerals from mine to markets, and provide services and facilities for truckers and traders alike. Significantly, the Government of Afghanistan also benefits, by gaining (through tariffs) a sustainable income stream. Let me remind you that today US taxpayers are paying all civil service salaries in Afghanistan.

Returning to our main question, is it wise or simply wrong to pay off Taliban forces to enable goods to pass through territories they control. My answer would be this: if this is simply to enable us to deliver military-related goods, it is wrong. It advertises our weakness without bringing direct benefits to the local population.

However, if such a policy is part of a larger strategy based on the reopening of transport and trade within and across Afghanistan, it is prudent and wise. For people who see the chance of getting their crops to higher-priced markets will seize them. They will fight anyone who proposes to close the road thereafter. Similarly, people who are profiting from feeding and servicing the transport sector will resist anyone who proposes to shut down road transport, or to resist the construction of railroads or pipelines. Seen in this context, *paying Taliban to keep open a road is nothing less than a way of hiring the Taliban to work towards their own demise.*

The Government of Afghanistan fully understands this, and therefore supports the strategy proposed here. Hamid Karzai has written:

> "...Once we are on our feet with our own economy,...with Afghanistan becoming a hub for transportation in Central Asia and South and West Asia..., Afghanistan will remain a strong and good and economically viable partner with the United States and our other allies."

In the same spirit, General David H. Petraeus writes: that:

> "Sound strategy demands the use of all the instruments of power. This vision for Afghanistan and the region makes a compelling case that transport and trade can help restore the central role of Afghanistan in Central Asia. By once again becoming a transport hub, Afghanistan can regain economic vitality and thrive as it did in the days of the Silk Road."

CHAPTER SOURCES

The following chapters have been previously published:

Chapter 1 – This is an edited, excerpted and augmented edition of a United States House of Representatives publication, dated June 2010.

Chapter 2 – These remarks were delivered as Statement of John F. Tierny before the U.S. House of Representatives Committee on Oversight and Government Reform, given June 22, 2010.

Chapter 3 – These remarks were delivered as Statement of Lieutenant General William N. Phillips before the U.S. House of Representatives Committee on Oversight and Government Reform, given June 22, 2010.

Chapter 4 – These remarks were delivered as Statement of Gary Motsek before the U.S. House of Representatives Committee on Oversight and Government Reform, given June 22, 2010.

Chapter 5 – These remarks were delivered as Statement of Brigadier General John W. Nicholson before the U.S. House of Representatives Committee on Oversight and Government Reform, given June 22, 2010.

Chapter 6 - These remarks were delivered as Statement of Moshe Schwartz before the U.S. House of Representatives Committee on Oversight and Government Reform, given June 22, 2010.

Chapter 7 – These remarks were delivered as Statement of Carl Forsbergh before the U.S. House of Representatives Committee on Oversight and Government Reform, given June 22, 2010.

Chapter 8 – These remarks were delivered as Statement of Dr. T. X. Hammes before the U.S. House of Representatives Committee on Oversight and Government Reform, given June 22, 2010.

Chapter 9 – These remarks were delivered as Statement of S. Frederick Starr before the U.S. House of Representatives Committee on Oversight and Government Reform, given June 22, 2010.

INDEX

A

B

C

D

E

F

G